Tibet

Tibet

BY LIZ SONNEBORN

Enchantment of the World™
Second Series

CHILDREN'S PRESS®

An Imprint of Scholastic Inc.

Frontispiece: **Mythological figure as roof decoration at Jokhang Temple**

Consultant: Nicole Willock, PhD, Assistant Professor, Department of Philosophy and Religious Studies, Old Dominion University, Norfolk, Virginia

Please note: All statistics are as up-to-date as possible at the time of publication.

Book production by The Design Lab

Library of Congress Cataloging-in-Publication Data
Names: Sonneborn, Liz, author.
Title: Tibet / by Liz Sonneborn.
Description: New York : Children's Press, a division of Scholastic [2016] |
   Series: Enchantment of the world | Includes bibliographical references and index.
Identifiers: LCCN 2015048619 | ISBN 9780531218884 (library binding)
Subjects: LCSH: Tibet Autonomous Region (China) —Juvenile literature.
Classification: LCC DS786 .S667 2016 | DDC 951/.5—dc23
LC record available at http://lccn.loc.gov/2015048619

1 2 3 4 5 6 7 8 9 10 R 26 25 24 23 22 21 20 19 18 17

Tibetan in traditional dress

Contents

Left to right: **Yarlung Tsangpo River, farmers, King Gesar, prayer flags, boys**

CHAPTER 1

Fighting for a Free Tibet

IN 1937, A GROUP OF BUDDHIST MONKS TRAVELED to a small village in what is now the Qinghai Province of China. They came to see a two-year-old boy named Lhamo Dondrup, the son of poor parents who eked out a living by farming a small plot of land. The monks showed the child several objects. They asked him which of the objects belonged to him. Lhamo Dondrup pointed to a string of prayer beads, a walking stick, and a drum. The monks were relieved. After an exhausting search, they had finally found what they were looking for. Little Lhamo Dondrup, they believed, was the new Dalai Lama, the political and spiritual leader of the Asian country of Tibet.

The religion of Tibetan Buddhism teaches that, after death, humans are reincarnated, or reborn as different beings. Several years before the monks' quest, Thubten Gyatso, the thirteenth

Opposite: **Buildings cling to the hillsides in the rugged mountains of Tibet.**

As a young boy, Tenzin Gyatso spoke a dialect, or version, of Chinese. He did not learn Tibetan until later.

Dalai Lama had died. The monks had since been scouring the countryside looking for his next incarnation. Their search eventually led them to Lhamo Dondrup's village. The boy had certain physical characteristics—such as upward-slanting eyes and large ears—that the monks expected a Dalai Lama to have. But only after the boy picked out the personal possessions of the deceased Dalai Lama were they sure that he was the reincarnation of their former leader.

Living in Exile

When Lhamo Dondrup was four, he was taken to Lhasa, the capital of Tibet. At a ceremony at the Potala Palace, he received the name Tenzin Gyatso. In the years that followed, he received rigorous training to prepare him for the important role he would soon take on. His tutors taught him about logic, medicine, and Tibetan art and culture. He also studied Buddhist religious practices and philosophy.

Usually, a Dalai Lama takes over leadership of Tibet when he turns eighteen. But Tenzin Gyatso received power over the country in 1950, when he was just fifteen years old. Tibet was in turmoil. Late that year, soldiers from China, Tibet's neighbor to the north and east, had crossed the border into Tibet. By the next year, Chinese forces had taken over Lhasa. The Chinese government declared that Tibet was not an independent nation. It said that Tibet was now and always had been part of China.

Chinese troops march toward the Tibetan border in 1950.

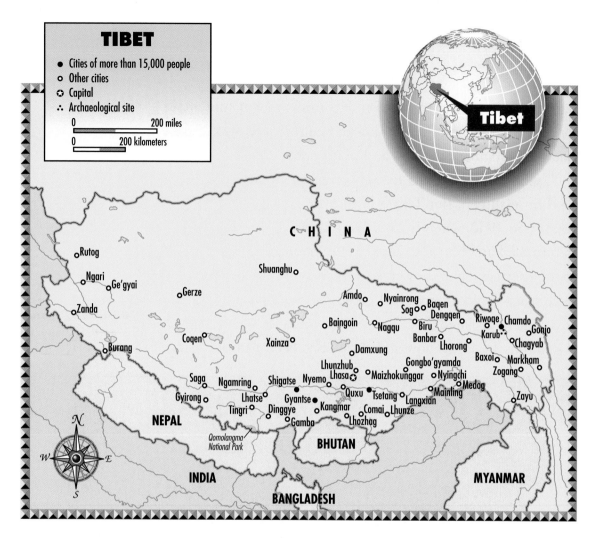

TIBET

- ● Cities of more than 15,000 people
- ○ Other cities
- ✧ Capital
- ∴ Archaeological site

0   200 miles

0   200 kilometers

Tibet

CHINA

Rutog

Ngari

Ge'gyai

Zanda

Gerze

Shuanghu

Amdo

Nyainrong

Sog   Baqen

Dengqen

Riwoqe   Chamdo

Gonjo

Baingoin

Nagqu

Biru

Karub

Chagyab

Coqen

Xainza

Banbar

Lhorong

Baxoi

Markham

Burang

Damxung

Gongbo'gyamda

Nyingchi

Zogang

Lhunzhub

Saga

Ngamring

Shigatse

Nyemo

Lhasa

Maizhokunggar

Medog

Zayu

Gyirong

Lhatse

Quxu

Tsetang

Langxian

Mainling

Tingri

Dinggye

Gyantse

Kangmar

Comai

Lhunze

Lhozhag

Gamba

Qomolangma National Park

NEPAL

INDIA

BHUTAN

BANGLADESH

MYANMAR

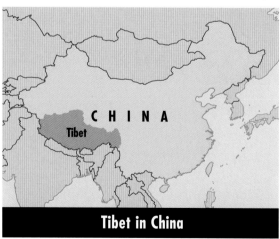

CHINA

Tibet

Tibet in China

The new Dalai Lama attempted to engage China in peace talks, with little success. At the same time, the Tibetan people became increasingly resentful of the Chinese presence in their homeland. After years of resistance, they staged a full-scale rebellion in 1959, which the Chinese army quickly put down. Knowing his life was in danger, the Dalai Lama, disguised as a soldier, fled from Tibet. He crossed the Himalaya mountain chain into India. There, he established a Tibetan government in exile in the town of Dharamsala.

Building Support

For decades, the Dalai Lama has fought to free Tibetans from Chinese rule. He initially demanded that Tibet receive its full independence. But in 1979 he moderated his position. Since then, he has advocated what he calls the "middle way." The Dalai Lama is now willing to allow Tibet to be part of China, as long as Tibet's religion, culture, and language are protected.

The Dalai Lama is a major world figure. Here, he greets a crowd in Frankfurt, Germany.

The Dalai Lama has proven himself extremely skilled at promoting this cause, especially to people in North America and Europe. Lecturing widely and visiting world leaders, he became famous for his calm demeanor, wise words, and charismatic personality. For his efforts to find a nonviolent solution to the conflict between Tibet and China, he was awarded the Nobel Peace Prize in 1989.

Worldwide, the Dalai Lama has become an esteemed figure, one of the world's most beloved spiritual leaders. His widespread popularity was particularly evident in the outpouring of affection for him in 2015 on his eightieth birthday. His birthday was celebrated at many events in different countries. One of the

The Dalai Lama takes part in one of his many eightieth birthday celebrations at an event in California.

largest was held in New York City on July 11, with more than fifteen thousand people crowding into an auditorium to see him. With his round glasses and kind smile, the Dalai Lama sat quietly on the stage as a parade of speakers paid tribute to him. "Very few other people have made such a positive contribution to humanity as His Holiness with the unwavering message of compassion," said Valerie Jarrett, a senior advisor to President Barack Obama. When she called him "an extraordinary leader, a good man, a man with amazing grace," the audience burst into applause.

Lhasa has been the religious center of Tibet since the ninth century CE. Its name means "home of the gods."

Banned in His Native Land

In Tibet, however, there were no public celebrations. The streets, in fact, were full of soldiers and police determined to put an end to any acknowledgment of the birthday or even of the Dalai Lama himself. Today, any Tibetan who speaks

A Tibetan in Dharamsala, India, prays at a ceremony commemorating the fiftieth anniversary of the Dalai Lama being forced to leave Tibet.

his name in public can expect to be punished. Anyone who displays his picture is likely to be arrested.

In the past, China had engaged in talks with the Dalai Lama, but in 2010, China ended all communications with him. The Chinese government accuses the Dalai Lama of promoting violent protest. It rejects the popular image of the Dalai Lama as an agent of peace. Chinese officials have instead called him a "devil with the face of a human but the heart of a beast."

Despite China's hostility toward the Dalai Lama, the people of Tibet continue to revere him. Many people ignore the ban on his image and secretly keep a portrait of him hidden in their homes. That devotion only helps to fuel the anger of the Chinese officials. They fear that as long as Tibetans look to the Dalai Lama for spiritual guidance, China's hold on Tibet will be in danger.

The Next Dalai Lama

The Dalai Lama's eightieth birthday not only sparked celebrations worldwide. It also furthered speculation about who will choose the aging leader's successor when he dies. In the past, the answer was clear. Select monks would head out in search of his reincarnated self. When the current Dalai Lama dies, however, the process of finding the next one will likely be more complicated. The Chinese government has already signaled that it wants to name the fifteenth Dalai Lama. Its candidate would undoubtedly support the Chinese regime and its goals for Tibet.

Aware of China's plans, the fourteenth Dalai Lama has suggested to his followers that perhaps the position should end with his death. In a 2014 interview, the Dalai Lama said, "There is no guarantee that some stupid Dalai Lama won't come next, who will disgrace himself or herself. That would be very sad. So, much better that a centuries-old tradition should cease at the time of a quite popular Dalai Lama."

Since China's invasion of Tibet, Tibetans have resisted Chinese rule. Protests in Tibet have mostly been nonviolent, however, in large part because of the Dalai Lama. But after his death, especially if the Chinese insist on installing his successor, the long simmering tensions in Tibet might reach a boiling point. At the very least, the selection of the new Dalai Lama will focus the world's attention on a question that has dominated much of Tibetan history: Who will determine the course of Tibet's future—the Chinese government or the Tibetan people themselves?

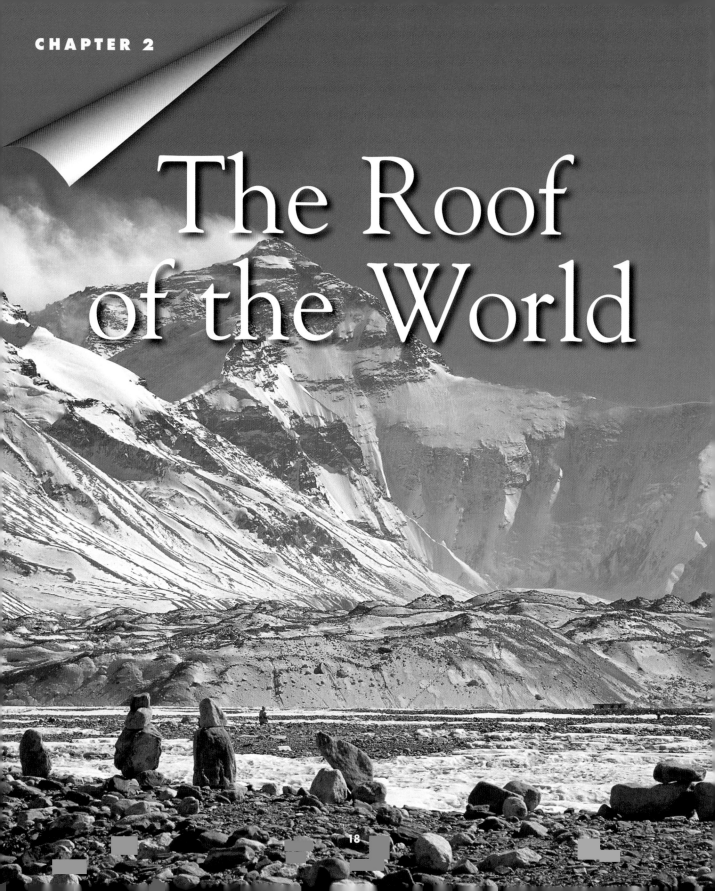

CHAPTER 2

The Roof of the World

AMONG THE MANY DISAGREEMENTS BETWEEN THE Tibetans and Chinese is the very definition of the word *Tibet*. To the Chinese, Tibet is the Tibet Autonomous Region (TAR). This area within the southwestern border of China stretches over 471,662 square miles (1,221,600 square kilometers). The TAR shares an international boundary with Myanmar, India, Bhutan, and Nepal to the south. (In several areas, however, Tibet's border is in dispute, with both China and India laying claim to certain lands.) To the east are the Chinese provinces of Qinghai, Sichuan, and Yunnan. To the north is the Xinjiang Uyghur Autonomous Region, which is also part of China.

The TAR covers about one-fifth of China's land area. It is a little larger than the U.S. states of Texas and California

Opposite: **Mount Everest towers above the Tibetan Plateau. The border between Nepal and the Tibet Autonomous Region of China runs exactly along its summit.**

Xinjiang Uyghur
Autonomous Region

Gansu
Province

C H I N A

D o - t o d

Qinghai Province

C h a n g T a n g

Dharamsala

Tibet Autonomous Region

D o - m e d

Sichuan
Province

U - T s a n g

Lhasa

NEPAL

BHUTAN

INDIA

MYANMAR

Yunnan
Province

Cultural Tibet

combined. In the view of many Tibetans, however, the TAR is just a portion of what they consider Tibet. They believe Tibet is about twice the size of the TAR and includes parts of four Chinese provinces (Qinghai, Sichuan, Yunnan, and Gansu). These areas were traditionally inhabited by Tibetans and were thought to be part of Tibet before the Chinese seized control of the country in 1950. Tibet, defined in this way, is often referred to as Cultural Tibet.

Mountains and Rivers

For much of its history, Tibet was one of the most isolated places in the world, largely because of its geography. Its lands are located on an extremely high plateau surrounded by mountain ranges. These mountains have long discouraged all

Tibet's Geographic Features

Area (Tibet Autonomous Region): 471,662 square miles (1,221,600 sq km)

Area (Cultural Tibet): 965,255 square miles (2,500,000 sq km)

Highest Elevation: Mount Everest (called Jomolungma in Tibet), 29,035 feet (8,850 m) above sea level

Largest Lake: Namtso, 740 square miles (1,917 sq km)

Longest River: Yangtze, 3,915 miles (6,301 km) through China

Deepest Canyon: Yarlung Tsangpo Grand Canyon, 17,657 feet (5,382 m)

Average High Temperature: June, 82°F (28°C)

Average Low Temperature: December, 9°F (-13°C)

Average Annual Rainfall: 5 to 15 inches (13 to 38 cm)

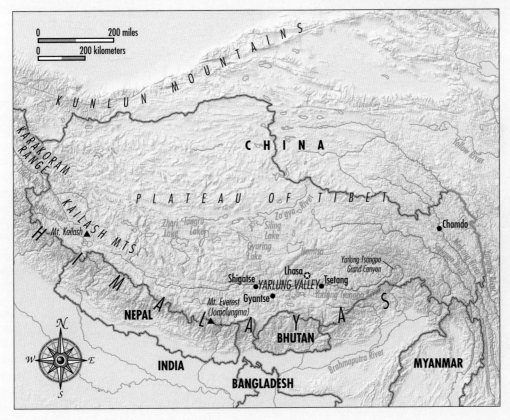

A Tibetan nomad herds horses on the Tibetan Plateau. The world's highest plateau, it has an elevation of about 3 miles (5 km) above sea level.

but the most determined foreigners from entering the region. The Tibetan plateau on average is about 15,000 feet (4,600 meters) above sea level. Less than 5 percent of Tibet's lands lie below 8,000 feet (2,400 m). Because of its high elevation, Tibet has been nicknamed the Roof of the World.

The mountains around the plateau, of course, rise far higher. The Kunlun Mountains are located to the north, and the Karakoram are found to the west. But the greatest peaks lie in the Himalayas, located to the south along Tibet's border with Nepal. The Himalayas boast the highest mountain in the world, Mount Everest (known as Jomolungma to the people of Tibet), which rises to 29,035 feet (8,850 meters) above sea level. In 2012, China established Qomolangma National Park in the region surrounding Mount Everest. It is the world's highest national park.

Another notable peak in Tibet is Mount Kailash in the Kailash mountain range, which runs parallel to the Himalayas. It is considered a sacred site by several religions, including Buddhism and Hinduism.

Naming Everest

To the Tibetans, it was Jomolungma, or "Goddess Mother." To the Nepalese, it was Sagarmatha, or "Head of the Sky." But in 1865, the towering mountain located along the border of Tibet and Nepal received a new and much less poetic name: Mount Everest.

In 1852, Radhanath Sikdar, an Indian mathematician, identified this mountain in the Himalayas as the highest in the world. The British, who then controlled India, pored over Sikdar's calculations for four years before they announced that it was in fact the world's highest peak. The British government renamed the mountain Mount Everest, after George Everest, who had earlier headed the British survey that had mapped India. In addition to honoring Everest, the British changed the mountain's name so it would be easier for English-speakers to pronounce.

Many of the greatest rivers in Asia have their source in Tibet. They include the Brahmaputra, the Salween, the Mekong, and China's two longest rivers—the Yangtze, and the Yellow. Tibet is also dotted with lakes. Its largest salt lake is called Namtso. A popular tourist destination, Namtso, with its clear turquoise waters backed by snowcapped mountains, offers some of the most beautiful scenery in the region.

Varied Environments

The northern part of the Tibetan plateau, called the Chang Tang, has the country's most forbidding environment. Making up about one-third of Tibet, it is largely cold and barren, with no rivers at all, although it does have some salty lakes. Even in the summer, heavy snowfall is common. More comfortable are the forest areas in the east. Most people in Tibet live in the southern region, north of the Himalayas, where river valleys provide fertile farmland. Most of Tibet's towns and cities, including the capital of Lhasa, are located there.

India and Nepal, on the southern side of the Himalayas, are soaked by rain carried by monsoon winds each summer.

A woman walks along the shore of Namtso Lake. The lake's name means "Heavenly Lake," which could refer to either its legendary beauty or its elevation.

Tibetan women pitch straw during the barley harvest. The barley straw is used as animal feed, while the grain is a staple for the people of Tibet.

But the high Himalayas block Tibet from these intense winds. As result, Tibet is a relatively dry region. It usually receives only about 5 to 15 inches (13 to 38 centimeters) of rainfall a year. Tibet also experiences very little humidity. In fact, the air is so dry that grain can be stored for up to fifty years without spoiling.

Temperatures in Tibet vary greatly. Depending on the region, they can rise as high as 90 degrees Fahrenheit (32 degrees Celsius) in the summer or drop as low as –40°F (–40°C) in the winter. But in the most populated areas of Tibet, temperatures are fairly mild. At Lhasa, Tibet's capital, high temperatures in June and July reach about 73°F (23°C). Low temperatures in December and January fall to about 18°F (–8°C). Because of Tibet's high elevation, temperatures sometimes fluctuate wildly in a single day. In the summer, for example, in some areas temperatures can rise to 80°F (27°C) at noon and then fall below freezing at midnight.

Tibetan monks walk through a snowy courtyard in a monastery.

The Cities of Tibet

Tibetans are largely a rural people, but in recent years, a growing number have become city dwellers. Most urban Tibetans live in Lhasa, the capital of Tibet, which has a population of about 400,000. But the populations of the region's other cities and towns are also on the rise.

Shigatse (called Rikaze in Chinese) is Tibet's second-largest city, home to about 80,000 people. In 2014, a new railway opened in Shigatse that provides a direct route from the city to Beijing, the Chinese capital. Shigatse's best-known landmark is the Tashilhunpo Monastery (below). Gendun Drup, the first Dalai Lama, founded it in 1447. For hundreds of years, it was occupied by the Panchen Lama, who was Tibet's second most-powerful religious leader. The monastery houses an 85-foot-tall (26 m) statue of Jampa, or Maitreya, a future Buddha. This figure is revered by Tibetan Buddhists. The statue was crafted in the year 1914 by one thousand artisans out of about 600 pounds (270 kilograms) of gold.

Chamdo (right), in far eastern Tibet, also has a population of about 80,000. It was invaded by China in October 1950. Its fall was the beginning of the end of Tibet's history as an independent nation. The Chinese government has recently built up the area in hopes of making it into a business center. Nearby, the Karub Ruins are a popular tourist attraction. The ruins feature the remains of a Tibetan village from four thousand years ago.

Legend holds that the first Tibetan people were born at the site of the modern city of Tsetang, now home to 52,000 people. Its most famous landmark is the

Ganden Monastery. Samye, the first monastery in Tibet, is also located nearby. It was founded in the eighth century and has been restored many times. It is a major tourist and pilgrimage destination today.

The town of Gyantse (left), which has a population of 15,000, has long been an important center for trade. Beginning in the seventeenth century, Tibetan traders met Indian and Nepalese merchants at Gyantse to barter their wares. The town is also known for its textiles, particularly its high-quality woven carpets. Visitors to Gyantse often tour the Pelkhor Chödé Monastery, built in the 1430s, and the ruins of the Dzong Fort. The fort was destroyed during the British invasion of Tibet in the early twentieth century.

CHAPTER 3

In the Wild

PEOPLE OFTEN FEEL A SPECIAL CONNECTION TO THE plants and animals living among them. For most Tibetans, having a close relationship to the natural world is also part of their religious beliefs. Buddhism, the religion of nearly all Tibetans, promotes compassion for all living things and deep respect for the habitats in which they live. In Tibet, Buddhists seek to follow the Dalai Lama's frequent calls for them to be good caretakers of the earth and its creatures.

Opposite: **Spruces, firs, larches, pines, birches, and many other trees grow in the forests of Tibet.**

Plant Life

With Tibet's high altitude and often forbidding landscapes, most plants that survive must be hardy. The northern plateau has the most challenging environment for plant life. Its vegetation is limited to grasses and a few small shrubs.

Lands to the east and the south, however, are covered with trees. These areas have the densest forests in all of China. Oaks, birches, elms, poplars, and teak are just a few of the tree varieties found in Tibet.

The most hospitable regions for plant life are the river valleys of southern Tibet. This area is also the center for agriculture. Farmers grow barley, buckwheat, and other food crops

Oat plants sway in the wind in a fertile valley in southern Tibet.

The Blue Poppy

In the wet, mountainous region of southeastern Tibet grows the Himalayan blue poppy. The plant is not actually a true poppy, although it resembles one. But the blue in its name is certainly accurate. Its brilliant blooms have a brighter blue color than any other flower. While these plants flourish in Tibet, they are very hard to grow elsewhere. Still, many gardeners around the world have taken up the challenge, often without success, to cultivate these colorful and coveted flowering plants.

there. Orchards of fruit trees in the region provide Tibetans with peaches, apricots, apples, and pears.

In the spring and summer, many varieties of colorful wildflowers bloom. Common flowers in eastern river valleys include daisies, irises, and buttercups. Himalayan edelweiss and poppies grow at higher elevations. Even in the inhospitable grasslands, several species of wildflowers thrive. In warmer months, red lilies and pink and white jasmine flowers fill the bleak environment with color.

Beasts of Tibet

Tibet was once teaming with wild animals, both large and small. For much of its history, it was isolated from the rest of the world. Without modern development, its animal population was largely undisturbed by human activities. Only recently, as China has constructed highways and rail lines into Tibet, have wild animals been pushed out of their natural

Symbol of Tibet

The mythical snow lion has been a symbol of Tibet since the early twentieth century. The white-furred beast represents strength and power. Before 1959, the fabled animal appeared on Tibet's stamps, coins, and banknotes. Two snow lions are still featured on the flag of the Central Tibetan Administration, Tibet's exile government in India. According to Tibetan folk songs, the snow lion lives on Tibet's highest mountains. The milk of the snow lioness is said to have special powers, and humans who drink it are promised a long life.

habitats. But in less populated and more remote areas, many species of animals can still be spotted in the wild.

Tibet is home to more than 140 types of mammals. Small mammals include squirrels, mice, rats, bats, and moles. On the northern plateau, the little pika, a relative to the rabbit, is the most common animal. Pikas feast on the area's grasses. They also burrow into the ground to create warrens, where they can stay warm during patches of harsh weather. Because the warrens collect river water, pikas help control flooding.

Pikas are also the primary source of food for the Tibetan fox. This small fox has thick brown and gray fur on its back and white fur on its chest. Its most distinctive features are its almost square-shaped head, small ears, and narrow snout.

Among the larger mammals of the Tibetan plateau are wild asses, brown bears, and musk deer. The white-lipped deer is found only in this region. Named for the white markings around its mouth, the deer has thick hooves, which allow it to stay steady while climbing or walking on uneven ground. The

Tibetan antelope, also called the chiru, is well adapted to the area's high altitude. It has an especially large number of red blood cells, which ensure that its muscles get enough oxygen even at the highest climes.

Although their numbers are dwindling, wild yaks also roam the plateau. Weighing up to 1,800 pounds (800 kilograms), these sturdy animals have long, thick coats that keep them

A yak stands by a roadside in Tibet. A female yak is called a dri. The dri provides herders with milk.

Fur Burning

In January 2006, the Dalai Lama made a public statement, prevailing on the Tibetan people to stop wearing the furs of endangered animals. Tibetans have long worn furs and garments with fur trim. But in recent years, it became fashionable for wealthier Tibetans to don pelts of more exotic animals. Many, including tiger and leopard furs, were smuggled in from India. Urged on by environmentalists, the Dalai Lama told Tibetans that making clothing of these animals' furs violated Buddhist beliefs.

Many Tibetans not only stopped wearing furs. They also started burning the ones they already owned. At fur-burning events, people came together to throw their furs one by one on a fire. As each pelt was set aflame, the people shouted with joy. In just a few weeks, the Tibetan people had destroyed almost $65 million worth of furs.

Fur burning became a way for Tibetans to show their devotion both to Buddhism and to the Dalai Lama. The Chinese government, which sees the Dalai Lama as an enemy, banned fur burnings. It even began forcing Tibetans to wear furs at certain festivals. Anyone who looked unhappy about donning fur ran the risk of being beaten or arrested by the authorities.

warm in the most severe weather. Most yaks in Tibet, however, are now domesticated. For centuries, Tibetan nomads have made their living by caring for yak herds that feed off the grasslands. Yaks have also long been used as transportation

The Red Panda

The giant panda, the national animal of China, is a large, roly-poly creature about the size of a bear. But the red panda, native to southern Tibet, is an adorable, agile animal only slightly bigger than a house cat. It has thick red-orange fur and a fluffy striped black-tipped tail. Because of its short legs, the red panda walks slowly. But red pandas are skilled climbers and spend most of their time in trees. The red panda is now endangered, largely because Tibet's growing timber industry is destroying its habitats.

Snow leopards have stocky bodies and thick fur, which help keep them warm. Their broad paws help them walk on top of the snow.

and for carrying loads of goods over rugged terrain. In addition, the animals provide herders with milk, meat, wool, and dung, which people burn as fuel.

The forests of Tibet are also rich in wildlife. Tigers, lynx, jackals, and monkeys are all found there. Mountainous regions are home to snow leopards. These leopards are known by their light gray fur and dark gray spots, which act as camouflage on snowy mountainsides.

The golden pheasant is native to the forests of Tibet. These brightly colored birds grow about 3 feet (1 m) long, more than two-thirds of which is tail.

Birds, Reptiles, and Insects

There are more than four hundred species of birds in Tibet. They include geese, gulls, pheasants, larks, sparrows, crows, and cranes. Tibetans always welcome the sighting of a black-necked crane, which they consider sacred. The elegant bird spends the summer on the grasslands but migrates to agricultural lands to the south in winter. Vultures also play an important role in Tibetan culture. In Tibetan funeral rites, the corpse of a dead person is often left for vultures to feed on.

Dozens of types of reptiles, amphibians, and fish dwell in Tibet's varied habitats. They include snakes, lizards, turtles, frogs, and carp. Of the more than two thousand species of insects in Tibet, one of the most unusual is the Himalayan jumping spider. Found on the slopes of Mount Everest, it can survive at extremely high altitudes. The spider feeds on insects that are swept high up in the air by strong winds. Its eight eyes help the spider spot its airborne prey.

The black-necked crane is the only crane species that lives in the high mountains.

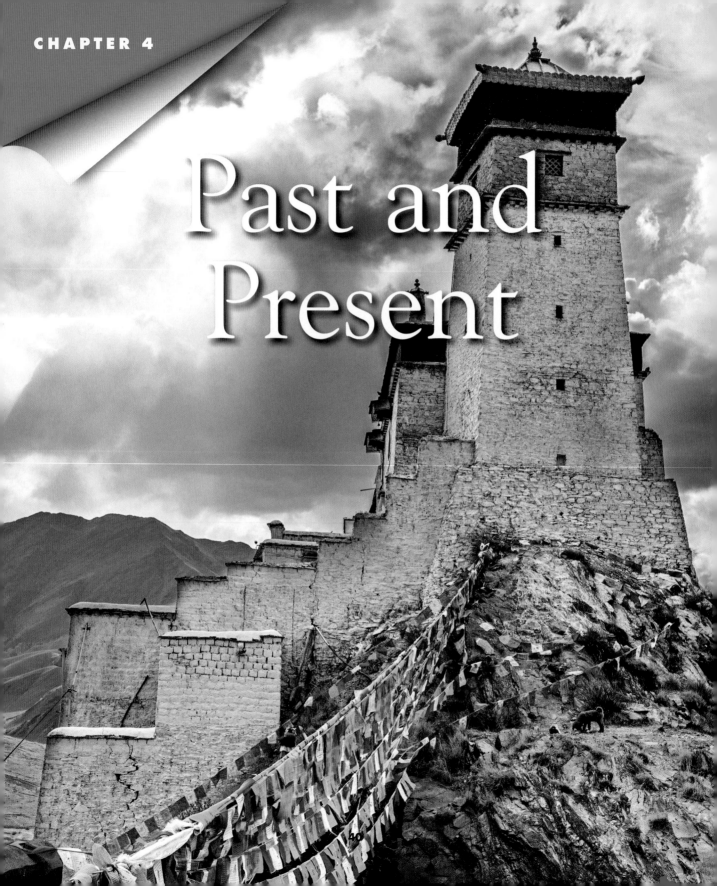

CHAPTER 4

Past and Present

THE EARLIEST HISTORY OF TIBET IS TOLD THROUGH ancient myths and legends. One tale recounts how a female ogre fell in love with the religious figure Avalokiteshvara, while he was in the form of a monkey. Their children are said to be the first Tibetans.

Another story tells of Nyatri Tsenpo, who is called the first king of Tibet. Said to have been born with blue eyebrows and webbed fingers, he was cast out of India by his father because of his strange appearance. Nyatri Tsenpo then wandered to the Yarlung Valley in southern Tibet. The farmers there asked him where he came from, but not speaking their language, he did not understand them. Nyatri Tsenpo pointed to the

Opposite: **According to legend, Yumbulagang Palace was the first building in Tibet and the palace of Tibet's king Nyatri Tsenpo.**

A Mythic King

The legendary King Gesar is a great hero in Tibet and Mongolia, to the north of China. Beginning in about the eleventh century, traveling storytellers entertained audiences with songs about his adventures. Gesar was the warrior king of a mythic kingdom called Ling in eastern Tibet. After obtaining supernatural weapons and marrying a beautiful wife, he was set upon by a series of evil enemies. His enemies succeeded in exiling him from Ling, but after wandering through the mountains, he returned, battled his foes, and restored peace and prosperity to his land. The stories about Gesar were eventually written down. Instead of just one accepted text, there are more than one hundred volumes that tell the epic tale of Gesar and his exploits.

sky, which the farmers took to mean he had descended from heaven. Believing him to be a god, they named him their king in 127 BCE. The day Nyatri Tsenpo took the throne is now celebrated each year as the first day of the Tibetan calendar.

The Rise of Buddhist Tibet

A number of different groups lived on the Tibetan plateau. Gradually, they formed alliances and became a kingdom. The most successful of the early kings of Tibet was Songtsen Gampo. During the seventh century CE, he was able to unify and expand the lands under his control, making Tibet more powerful. He also located his court in Lhasa, which has since served as Tibet's capital.

Hoping to stay on good terms with the king, the rulers

of neighboring present-day Nepal and China both sent princesses to Tibet to marry Songtsen Gampo. The two women brought with them elaborate statues of Siddhartha Gautama. Known also as Buddha, Gautama was a holy man who had lived in Nepal in the sixth and fifth centuries BCE. His teachings provided the basis for the religion of Buddhism. King Songtsen Gampo established the first Buddhist temples in Tibet. But outside of the royal court, most of his people still observed an older religion's tradition. Now known as Bon, this religion called on its followers to perform rituals to please gods and pacify demons.

After King Songtsen Gampo's death, the Tibetan kingdom remained a powerful force in the region. Under the rule of Trisong Detsen in the eighth century, the Tibetan army even managed to take over the Chinese capital of Chang'an (now the city of Xi'an). Trisong Detsen also tried to spread the Buddhist faith by inviting two Indian teachers—Shantarakshita and Padmasambhava—to his realm. The three men established at Samye the first Tibetan monastery. Monasteries were teaching centers where men called monks pledged to devote their lives to studying and preserving Buddhist knowledge, beliefs, and practices.

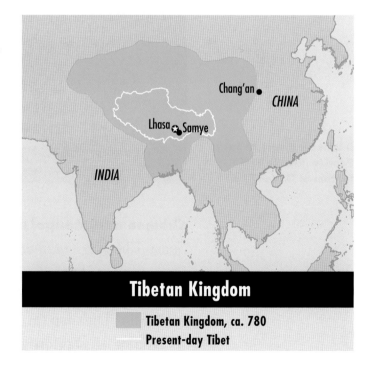

Tibetan Kingdom

▨ Tibetan Kingdom, ca. 780
— Present-day Tibet

A brass sculpture of Sakya Pandita, the spiritual teacher of Goden Khan

Chinese and Mongols

Some Tibetans remained opposed to Buddhism. In 838, Lang Darma, after the assassination of the sitting king, became Tibet's ruler. He was determined to restore the Bon faith in his lands. The new king destroyed temples and monasteries, and monks fled Tibet in terror. Lang Darma himself was assassinated by a monk in 841. With his death, Tibet fell into disarray. No one king was able to consolidate control over the region.

Tibet's power waned, leaving it vulnerable to foreigners. In the early thirteenth century, Genghis Khan, the leader of the Mongol people, took over China. Mongol soldiers, led by Genghis Khan's grandson Goden Khan, invaded Tibet in 1240. Goden Khan summoned Sakya Pandita, a great Tibetan scholar of Buddhism, to his court. Sakya Pandita granted Goden Khan authority over Tibet, and Goden Khan converted to Buddhism.

Chinese rulers of the Ming dynasty defeated the Mongol Yuan dynasty in the fourteenth century. While China believed it still had control over Tibet, actual power there fell to Buddhist religious leaders called lamas. The highest ranking was known as the Dalai Lama. The word *dalai* means "ocean" in the Mongolian language, suggesting the great depth of the Dalai Lama's spiritual faith and wisdom.

The most powerful of the early Dalai Lamas was Ngawang Lozang Gyatso, the fifth man to hold the title. He united the country under his leadership and constructed the

Mongol Conquest of Tibet

- Mongol Empire, 1240
- Added to Mongol Empire by 1259
- Present-day Tibet

Potala Palace in Lhasa. It became the official residence of future Dalai Lamas. The fifth Dalai Lama also created the office of the Panchen Lama, which he bestowed on his tutor. Since then, the Panchen Lama has been Tibet's second most influential religious and political leader.

Foreign Threats

In the centuries following Ngawang Lozang Gyatso's death, Dalai Lamas exerted less control over Tibet. Representatives from China held some sway, but Tibet, geographically isolated by its many mountain ranges, remained largely free of foreign influence. By the late nineteenth century, however, the growing British and Russian Empires were vying for dominance

The Potala Palace

Situated at the highest point of Lhasa, the Potala Palace is the traditional winter home of the Dalai Lama. At the site, King Songtsen Gampo built a royal residence in the seventh century, but invaders later destroyed it. The Potala Palace that now stands in its place was constructed in the seventeenth century during the rule of the powerful fifth Dalai Lama. Constructed by seven thousand laborers and 1,500 artists, it took almost fifty years to build. The structure includes two sections—the White Palace, completed in 1645, and the Red Palace, completed in 1693. The building stands thirteen stories high and has more than a thousand rooms. After the fourteenth Dalai Lama fled Tibet in 1959, the Chinese government turned the vast palace into a museum.

in central Asia. Wanting to stay outside of their sway, Tibet banned all foreigners from entering the country.

The British controlled India, however, and were eager to establish a trade relationship with Tibet. At the same time, they wanted to block Russia from gaining control over the country. With both these aims in mind, the British sent an expedition of some one thousand soldiers into Tibet in 1904. Tibet's defenses were so weak that it could not repel the invaders. About a thousand Tibetans died in the invasion, and the

In 1904, British troops entered Tibet to force the Tibetans to supply them with grain.

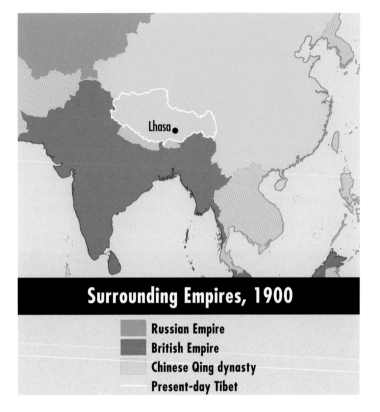

Surrounding Empires, 1900

Lhasa

- Russian Empire
- British Empire
- Chinese Qing dynasty
- Present-day Tibet

British easily captured Dzong Fort at the town of Gyantse. Leaders in Lhasa were forced to agree to become trading partners with the British.

Alarmed by the British assault on Tibet, China staged a military invasion in 1910 to re-exert control there. But the next year, the people of China revolted against their leaders, and the troops were withdrawn. With the overthrow of the Qing dynasty of emperors, China officially became the Republic of China in 1912.

In 1913, Thubten Gyatso, the thirteenth Dalai Lama, declared that Tibet was an independent nation, even though China still maintained that Tibet was part of its territory. Chinese forces did, in fact, control much of the eastern lands that the Dalai Lama claimed. But the rest of Tibet was effectively ruled by the Dalai Lama.

The thirteenth Dalai Lama died in 1933. Five years after his death, Tibetan religious leaders determined that a two-year-old boy named Lhamo Dondrup was the reincarnation of the former leader. The boy was renamed Tenzin Gyatso and taken to Lhasa, where he began his training to serve as the fourteenth Dalai Lama.

Mao Zedong was the leader of China for almost thirty years.

The Chinese Invade

While the new Dalai Lama was growing up, China fell into civil war. In 1949, forces under a man named Mao Zedong were victorious. Mainland China, ruled by Mao, was renamed the People's Republic of China (PRC). The PRC became a communist country. Under a communist system, the government controls all businesses and distributes income and property to its citizens. Communism, in theory, creates a fair society. But in practice, in China, it produced a repressive environment, where few people apart from Communist Party leaders had much personal freedom.

Soon after coming to power, Mao announced his intention to reestablish China's control over Tibet. When he ordered troops into Tibet in October 1950, he refused to say he was acting against the wishes of the Tibetan people. Mao instead insisted he was "liberating" Tibet from the influence of foreign governments and reabsorbing Tibet into China where it rightfully belonged.

A Tibetan with his yaks in the mid-twentieth century.

Mao's troops easily entered Tibet, which was not prepared to mount a military defense of its borders. Within months, the Chinese army had reached the capital of Lhasa. Tibetan leaders were forced to sign the Seventeen Point Agreement. The document designated Tibet a self-governing region within China, although it was actually under the strict control of the Chinese government. The agreement also allowed China's military to occupy the country.

China promised that it would turn Tibet into a modern nation. At the time, Tibet was very poor. Most people lived as peasant farmers and herders. Only the lamas and other members of the ruling class had any wealth. Modern conveniences, such as telephones, automobiles, and indoor plumbing were virtually unknown.

China built roads and constructed buildings from steel and concrete in Tibet. It brought electricity to the region. Some Tibetans supported China's efforts to modernize their nation, particularly because China initially promised not to interfere with Tibetan culture and religious practices. China even sponsored public ceremonies performed by lamas and monks.

Going into Exile

Soon after taking control, though, China became increasingly hostile to the Buddhist religion. Mao sought to repress all religious practices in China. He saw Tibetan Buddhism as a particular threat because of the political power of the Dalai Lama. In 1956, the Chinese authorities bombed several monasteries, an action that stunned the Tibetan people. Tensions

Ganden Monastery was destroyed during the rebellion of 1959. Then, in 1966, its remains were attacked during the Cultural Revolution.

between the Chinese and Tibetans became more and more heated before exploding in March 1959, when Tibetans staged a mass uprising. Chinese forces quickly crushed the rebellion. In the months that followed, they killed many Tibetans who opposed Chinese rule.

Fearing for his life, the twenty-four-year-old Dalai Lama fled the country, finding refuge in India. About eighty thousand other Tibetans, mostly people of high rank, also managed to escape Tibet and join him there. The Indian government offered them land, where the refugees set up farms and built monasteries. In the small town of Dharamsala, situated in the foothills of the Himalayas, the Dalai Lama founded a Tibetan government in exile. The Chinese government established the Tibet Autonomous Region (TAR) in 1965. Made up of lands formerly ruled by the Dalai Lama, the TAR had a governing structure similar to a Chinese province.

China's campaign against Tibetan Buddhism became even more inflamed during the Cultural Revolution of the 1960s and 1970s. During this period, young soldiers called the Red Guard stormed Tibet. They destroyed thousands of religious monuments and pieces of religious artwork. They also targeted monasteries, leaving them in ruins. Before the Cultural Revolution, there were about 2,700 monasteries in Tibet, but after these attacks only eight remained standing. The Red Guard also jailed monks throughout Tibet. Many of them did not survive their imprisonment. The Tibetan government in exile estimates that more than one million Tibetans died during the Cultural Revolution.

Grievances Against China

After Mao's death in 1976, China relaxed its assault on Tibetan Buddhism. While the government still persecuted religious leaders, it allowed for some monasteries and temples to be rebuilt. China also returned precious artwork that had been looted from Tibet. These more lenient Chinese government policies were put in place in part as a result of international pressure. By the 1980s, the plight of the Tibetan

Han women shop in Lhasa. People from the Han ethnic group own the majority of businesses in Lhasa.

people had become an important human rights issue in many Western nations.

Tibetan protests against the Chinese authorities continued throughout the 1980s and 1990s. China usually responded by setting down more restrictions on Tibetans' religious freedom, further angering the Tibetan people. Tibetans were also unhappy about the large number of Chinese immigrants in Tibet. The Chinese government was encouraging its people, particularly those of the Han ethnic group, the majority ethnic group in China, to relocate to Tibet. Many settled in the capital of Lhasa. Tibetans there became angry that these Han newcomers had better access to jobs, housing, and health care than they did.

The 2008 Uprising

On March 10, 2008, a group of monks from monasteries in Lhasa staged a protest march. It commemorated the forty-ninth anniversary of the 1959 Tibetan uprising. When the authorities arrested some of the marchers, many more Tibetans

The Disappearance of the Panchen Lama

One issue that has particularly inflamed Tibetans was the selection of the successor to the tenth Panchen Lama after his death in 1989. In 1995, the Dalai Lama and the Tibetan government in exile announced that a young boy named Gendun Chokyi Nyima was the reincarnation of the deceased religious leader. The Chinese authorities detained the boy and his family. They were never heard from again.

China then named its own Panchen Lama, Gyeltsen Norbu, who resides in the Chinese capital of Beijing. China sponsored a publicity campaign, designed to persuade the Tibetan people to accept Gyeltsen Norbu as the true Panchen Lama. But the campaign largely failed, as Tibetans became even more resentful of China's attempts to stifle their religious expression.

In 2008, Tibetan monks in India and other parts of the world held demonstrations to show their support for protesters in Tibet.

joined the protest. The uprising soon spread throughout the Tibet Autonomous Region and into the Chinese provinces of Sichuan, Gansu, and Qinghai. As in past protests, the Tibetans demanded political independence from China and freedom to practice their own religion. But many also spoke out against the economic advantages given to the Han Chinese in Tibet. The protest turned violent as some protesters attacked Han people and burned the businesses they owned.

The unrest in Tibet infuriated the Chinese government. It was preparing to host the 2008 Summer Olympics in Beijing. China saw the games as an opportunity to impress the world as a modern, confident nation. The problems in Tibet, widely reported in Western newspapers, put a damper on what China had envisioned as a triumphant moment in its history.

The government came down hard on the protesters. It placed even more restrictions on monasteries and sent as many as one thousand monks to prison. Chinese soldiers patrolled Tibet's streets. Secret police infiltrated the monasteries, reporting back to the government about any overheard anti-China sentiments.

In recent years, many Tibetans have become angry about the heavy presence of Chinese soldiers in their land. They believe Tibet is now under military occupation. Despite their protests, China continues to ignore the religious, social, and political grievances the Tibetan people have with Chinese rule.

Chinese soldiers patrol Barkhor Square in Lhasa.

CHAPTER 5

Two Governments

ON SEPTEMBER 8, 2015, OUTSIDE THE POTALA PALACE, thousands of invited guests gathered to celebrate the fiftieth anniversary of the creation of the Tibet Autonomous Region (TAR). Dancers and musicians in traditional Tibetan garb performed, as schoolchildren looked on while waving Chinese flags. Men in colorful military dress marched in unison, and floats celebrating the achievements of China's Communist Party rolled by. Chinese politician Yu Zhengsheng spoke to the crowd, crediting the party for spearheading Tibet's economic growth. "During the past fifty years," he said, "the Chinese Communist Party and the Tibetan people have led the transformation from a backward old Tibet to a vibrant socialist new Tibet."

One group of people was conspicuously absent from this carefully crafted celebration of the "new Tibet"—the monks and lamas to whom the Tibetan people had looked for leadership for centuries. Since 1950, the Chinese government has

Opposite: **Chinese soldiers stand at attention during the 2015 celebration marking the fiftieth anniversary of the founding of the Tibet Autonomous Region.**

The Chinese and Tibetan Flags

Officially, the national flag of Tibet is that of the People's Republic of China. The Chinese flag has a red field, because the color is associated with the communist revolution. In the upper left of the flag is one large yellow star, with four smaller ones to its right. The large star stands for the Chinese Communist Party. The smaller stars represent the different social classes in China that the party claims came together under communist rule.

The Central Tibetan Administration, the exiled Tibetan government in India, has its own national flag. Designed by the thirteenth Dalai Lama, it features a glowing sun at its center with red and dark blue stripes radiating from it. The red stripes stand for the six groups to which the ancestors of the Tibetan people belonged. The blue stripes represent the sky.

Pictured below the sun is a snowy mountain representing Tibet. It is held up by two mythical animals called snow lions, which also clutch a precious jewel. A band of yellow on the top, bottom, and left side of the flag stands for the teachings of Buddha.

The Chinese have outlawed the display of the flag in Tibet. It remains, however, a popular emblem in the rest of the world for the Tibetan independence movement.

laid claim to Tibet. But many Tibetans around the world challenge their authority. They say the actual government of Tibet is found in India, where the Dalai Lama fled in 1959.

Under China

Despite the views of the Tibetan people, the Chinese government wields political control over Tibet. No country in the world recognizes Tibet as an independent nation. Instead,

第十二届全国人民代表大会第四次会议
西藏自治区代表团全体会议

in all international dealings, Tibet is regarded as part of the People's Republic of China.

For political purposes, China is divided into twenty-three provinces, which are similar to states in the United States or provinces in Canada. There are also four municipalities (cities) and five autonomous regions—including the TAR—that function much like provinces. These areas are further divided into prefectures and counties.

According to the constitution of China, ethnic minorities in areas where they make up most of the population are supposed to run their own local governments. This rule applies to the TAR. It also applies in autonomous prefectures and counties in the Chinese provinces of Gansu, Qinghai, Sichuan, and Yunnan, in which the majority of people are ethnic Tibetans.

Lhasa has been Tibet's political and religious capital since the seventeenth century. The city traditionally was also an important trading center because of its location on trade routes connecting Tibet to its neighbors.

Lhasa is found in the southeastern portion of the Tibet Autonomous Region. Its name means "home of the gods." Lhasa, at an elevation of approximately 11,800 feet (3,600 m), is one of the highest cities in the world. Flanked by mountains, it has long been a difficult city to reach. In recent decades, China has constructed roads and railways to Lhasa, making it easier than ever to travel there.

The oldest section of Lhasa contains its most notable landmarks. In the city's center is the Jokhang Temple.

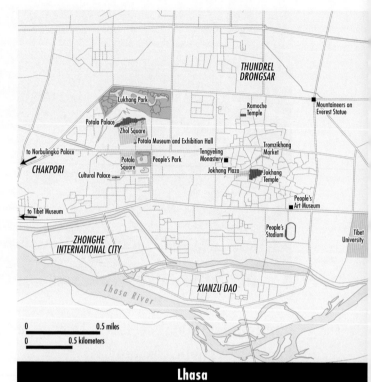

Lhasa

Every day, pilgrims gather there to worship. Tourists also flock to the gold-roofed structure to witness Buddhist rituals and shop in the lively stalls in the nearby market. The city is also home to the Potala Palace, which long served as the residence of the Dalai Lama, and several important monasteries.

More recently built areas in western Lhasa seem like an entirely different city. The modern office buildings, apartment complexes, supermarkets, nightclubs, and shopping malls there cater to Lhasa's growing population of Han Chinese.

The word *autonomous* in the name Tibet Autonomous Region suggests that the Tibetans living in this area run their own government. But in practice, officials in Beijing, the Chinese capital, make all the important decisions about governing the TAR. In fact, throughout China, real political power is held by leading members of the Chinese Communist Party rather than the people and their representatives in government.

Governing the TAR

The TAR is supposedly headed by a chairman, who always has been of Tibetan heritage. Since 2013, Lozang Gyeltsen (Luosang Jiangcun in Chinese) has held this position. When taking office, he announced his support of the official Chinese position that Tibet is part of China and that the Dalai Lama is a dangerous traitor. Promising to fight the Dalai Lama's calls for reform in Tibet, he stated, "We will unswervingly protect the unity of the motherland and ethnic harmony . . . and maintain harmony and stability in Tibet." The statements were not surprising, because he would not be permitted to be chairman unless his public views were strictly pro-Chinese.

Despite his title, Lozang Gyeltsen has little control over the governance of the TAR. Real power rests with the Communist Party chief for the TAR. Since 2011, this position has been held by Chen Quanguo, who, like others who have held this post, is Han Chinese. Chen Quanguo, in turn, must answer to his superiors in the party in Beijing.

Members of the Central Tibetan Administration meet in Dharamsala, India.

On paper, the lawmaking body of the TAR is its People's Congress. This organization also sends representatives to the National People's Congress. But the policies enacted by these organizations are all crafted by Communist Party officials. As a result, the Tibetan people in the TAR, both on a local and national level, have very little say in the laws and priorities of their government.

The Central Tibetan Administration

Since the fourteenth Dalai Lama fled to India in 1959, two governments have laid claim to Tibet—the Chinese government and the Tibetan government in exile, now known as the Central Tibetan Administration (CTA). The CTA was founded by the Dalai Lama in Dharamsala, India.

According to the CTA, this government was modeled after the political system established by the powerful fifth Dalai Lama in the seventeenth century. In this old traditional Tibetan government, the Dalai Lama was the head of state. He was assisted by the Kashag, meaning "house of order." The Kashag was composed of several ministers called kalön, who were appointed by the Dalai Lama. The number of kalön varied, but the Kashag usually included both monks and people

Dharamsala sits in the forest in the foothills of the Himalayas.

who were not part of religious orders. The CTA also claims that its democratic structure has roots in the way ancient Tibetan kingdoms were governed. Although kings always had the final say, they consulted with their people about the issues that concerned them.

The CTA now operates under the Charter of the Tibetans in Exile. This constitution was adopted in 1991 and has been amended several times. Under the charter, the government of the CTA has three branches that share power—the executive, the legislative, and the judicial.

The Tibetan Anthem

In the Tibet Autonomous Region, the Chinese national anthem "Yiyongjun Jinxingqu" ("The March of the Volunteers") is played at official events. However, the Central Tibetan Administration (CTA), the Tibetan government in exile, has its own anthem known as the "Gyellu." Its music came from an old sacred song. The lyrics were written in about 1950 by Trijang Rinpoche, who was a tutor of the current Dalai Lama when he was a young man. The anthem celebrates the wisdom and compassion of Buddha.

An English translation of the anthem begins:

Let the radiant light shine of Buddha's wish-fulfilling gem teachings,

The treasure chest of all hopes for happiness and benefit in both secular life and liberation.

O Protectors who hold the jewel of the teachings and all beings, nourishing them greatly,

May the sum of your karma grow full.

The Sikyong and the Kashag

The executive branch of the CTA is now headed by the sikyong ("political leader"). The sikyong is assisted by the Kashag, which includes seven kalön. Each presides over a department assigned to deal with a certain set of issues. The seven departments of the CTA are Health, Education, Finance, Security, Home, Religion and Culture, and Information and International Relations.

Tibetans in Dharamsala vote for the sikyong in the CTA elections. An estimated 150,000 Tibetans live in exile around the world. Those who are at least eighteen years old can vote in the elections.

In 2011, Lobsang Sangay was elected sikyong, the political leader of the Central Tibetan Administration. Born in 1968, Sangay has never lived in Tibet. The son of Tibetan exiles, he grew up in poverty in a refugee camp in India. He studied at the University of Delhi before traveling to the United States to attend Harvard University. He was the first Tibetan to earn a law degree from Harvard Law School.

On a whim, Sangay decided to run for sikyong, and was surprised when he received 55 percent of the votes cast by some forty-nine thousand Tibetan exiles. Working from his office in Dharamsala, India, Sangay has adopted the "middle way" promoted by the Dalai Lama. Rather than seeking political independence for Tibet, Sangay wants Tibet to become a self-governing region within China. Some Tibetan exiles have criticized him for taking this moderate position.

Lobsang Sangay has had little success in persuading China to consider any reforms regarding Tibet. Chinese

officials cut off all negotiations with the Dalai Lama in 2010. They have also refused to meet with Lobsang Sangay to discuss Tibet's future.

Initially, the Dalai Lama suggested three candidates for each kalön position. The other members then picked one of the candidates for the job. The kalön also chose the sikyong. But beginning in 2001, the CTA started holding popular elections for the head of the state.

The Dalai Lama encouraged this movement toward a more democratic political structure. He was also eager to pass along his political responsibilities. In 2011, the Dalai Lama announced that he was stepping away entirely from his political role; that year, Lobsang Sangay was elected sikyong.

Central Tibetan Administration

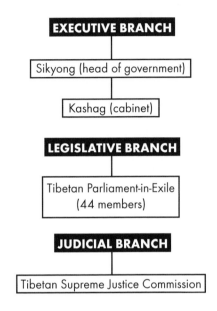

EXECUTIVE BRANCH

Sikyong (head of government)

Kashag (cabinet)

LEGISLATIVE BRANCH

Tibetan Parliament-in-Exile
(44 members)

JUDICIAL BRANCH

Tibetan Supreme Justice Commission

Any Tibetan exile who is at least eighteen years of age can vote for sikyong. The elected sikyong serves a term of five years. Among the sikyong's responsibilities is nominating the seven kalön, but candidates must be approved by the legislative branch before taking office.

Laws and Justice

The CTA's legislative body is the Tibetan Parliament-in-Exile. Its forty-four members are elected every five years. Ten members each represent U-Tsang, Do-tod, and Do-med, the three traditional provinces of Tibet. Two members each come from the four schools of Tibetan Buddhism and the Bon religion, which is based on the traditional religious beliefs of Tibet. Tibetans

Members of the Tibetan Parliament-in-Exile discuss issues during a break in their session. When the parliament is not in session, the members sometimes visit Tibetan settlements around the world to evaluate their conditions.

in Western countries are represented by four parliament members—two from Europe and two from North America.

The parliament meets in March and September for approximately two weeks. During these sessions, its members enact laws, oversee government spending, and consider candidates nominated to the Kashag. Throughout the year, they are also expected to tour settlements of exiles and ask people there about their problems and concerns. Tibetan exiles can also establish their own local parliaments. Thirty-eight local parliaments now serve large exile communities.

When members of the parliament disagree about the interpretation of a law, they turn to the CTA's judicial branch. It is headed by the Tibetan Supreme Justice Commission, which includes a chief justice commissioner. The members of this judicial body are selected by the parliament from a list of nominees presented by the Selection Committee, which includes the sikyong. The CTA's charter holds that members of the Tibetan Supreme Justice Commission must retire when they reach the age of sixty-five.

The Dalai Lama attends an event with members of the Tibetan government in exile.

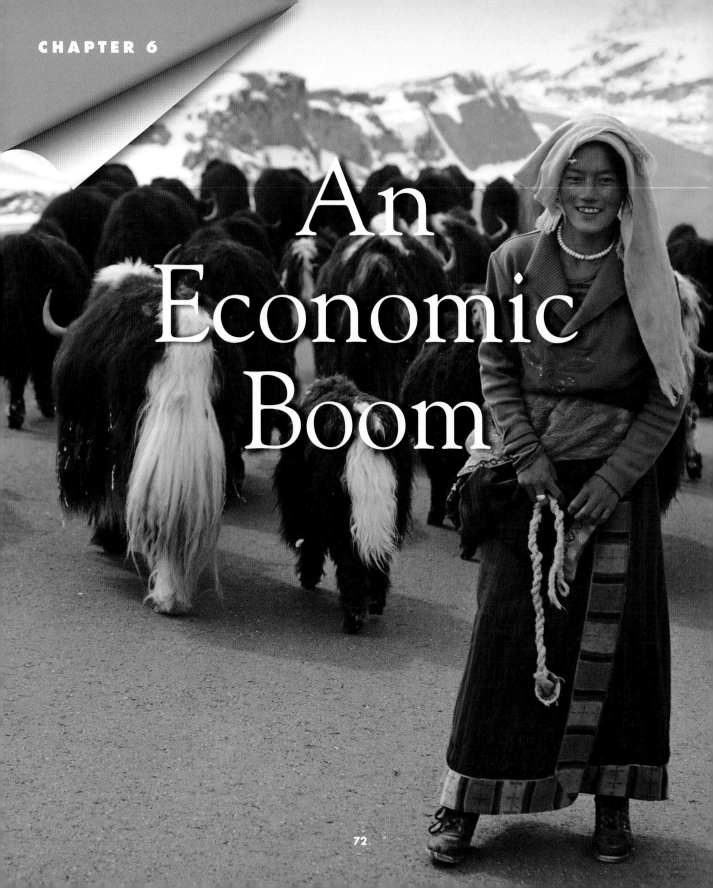

CHAPTER 6

An Economic Boom

UNTIL RECENTLY, NEARLY ALL TIBETANS MADE THEIR living the way their ancestors had—either by farming or by herding animals. Farmers largely lived along fertile river valleys. Their most important crop was a type of barley that thrived even in high elevations. Farmers also grew wheat, millet, beans, and hemp and raised animals such as cattle, sheep, chicken, and pigs.

Herders spent most of their time on the northern grasslands. There they raised yaks, sheep, and other livestock. Living in tents, they moved from place to place in search of new grazing areas where their animals could feed.

Some Tibetans earned their income by making traditional handicrafts. Such artisans included weavers, tanners, potters, and silversmiths. Often producing wares to sell to tourists, Tibetan artists were particularly known for their scroll paintings and their wood-block prints.

Opposite: **A woman herds yaks in the mountains of southern Tibet. Yaks, sheep, and goats are the most common livestock in the region.**

Tibetans use the money issued by the People's Republic of China (PRC). It is called renminbi, which means "people's money." The basic unit of currency is the yuan. Banknotes are issued in the amounts of 1, 5, 10, 20, 50, and 100 yuan. Also in use are coins worth 0.1 yuan, 0.5 yuan, and 1 yuan.

The front of all Chinese banknotes features a portrait of Mao Zedong, the leader who established the PRC. On the reverse side are images of landmarks. The Potala Palace is pictured on the 50-yuan note. Built by the fifth Dalai Lama, the palace is one of the most famous buildings in Tibet. In 2016, 1 Chinese yuan equaled US$0.15 and US$1 was worth 6.5 Chinese yuan.

Modernizing Tibet

Large numbers of Tibetans still make their living in these traditional professions. But in recent years, China has been trying to rapidly modernize Tibet's economy. Between 2001 and 2010 alone, it poured about $46 billion into Tibet. The Chinese government boasts that the economy of Tibet is growing at an incredibly fast rate, often by as much as 12 percent a year. In its communications with the outside world, China congratulates itself for everything it has done for Tibet.

Many Tibetans now enjoy a better standard of living than they had in the past. But the price of running water, television sets, and other goods has been high. Many did not abandon herding and farming by choice. Instead, they were forced off their land and left to live off small cash payments from the govern-

The Chinese have characterized the Tibetans of the past as peasants who were exploited by wealthy landowners. The typical Tibetan was poor, but Tibetans could usually feed themselves and their families. There is no evidence suggesting the Tibetan people suffered from a lack of food before 1950. Although poor, Tibetans generally enjoyed a fair amount of freedom, particularly in comparison to today. In addition, the fruits of their labor helped to build and sustain monasteries, which most workers, as devoted Buddhists, wanted to support.

ment. And despite China's claims, helping poor Tibetans is not the country's only goal in flooding money into Tibet's economy. The Chinese government itself stands to profit from these investments more than the Tibetan people.

Some Tibetan farmers still work in traditional ways.

Roads, Rail Lines, and Airports

As part of its modernizing efforts, China has spent huge sums of money to improve Tibet's transportation system. Before 1950, Tibetans generally traveled on well-worn paths, either on foot or on the back of a horse or other animal. Their most sophisticated forms of transportation were small boats made from wicker and animal hides. Long suspicious of outsiders, Tibetans were not interested in developing a modern transportation system that might bring more foreigners to their lands.

But after the Chinese took control, they immediately began building roads and highways. More recently, China has invested heavily in high-speed rail. In an amazing feat of engineering, the

Trains across Tibet travel through large stretches of unpopulated land with beautiful scenery.

government constructed a rail line between Beijing and Lhasa, making travel between the Chinese and Tibetan capitals easier than ever before.

Completed in 2006, this rail line is the highest in the world, in some places reaching elevations of more than 16,000 feet (4,900 m). The train cars have a special pressurized air system designed to allow passengers to breath at high elevations without feeling queasy. China has since built an extension that joins Lhasa to the Tibetan city of Shigatse. The government plans to further extend the line to the borders of India, Nepal, and Bhutan. China has also funded the construction of five airports in the Tibet Autonomous Region.

Making Sweaters

After the Dalai Lama fled Tibet for India, some eighty thousand Tibetans followed him into exile. The Tibetan government in India then faced the question of how these exiles could make a living. It encouraged the displaced Tibetans to make and sell a variety of handicrafts. One handicraft business—sweater making—proved particularly successful. Today, about 70 percent of the Tibetan exiles in India work in the sweater industry.

Many of these workers spend the summer weaving wool sweaters. When the weather cools, traders set up makeshift marketplaces to sell their wares. From October through January, sweater sellers operate about four hundred stalls in cities throughout India. When sweater season ends, they pack up and return home just in time for Losar, the traditional Tibetan New Year celebration.

So few cars travel on some Tibetan roads that travelers can sit in the middle of the road while taking a break.

Limiting Travel

China is extremely proud of the infrastructure improvements in Tibet. But Tibetans have been less enthusiastic about China's transportation development in their land. The new roads have made travel inside Tibet easier. But, since the mass anti-Chinese protests of 2008, China has strictly controlled the movements of Tibetans in their own land. Any Tibetan traveling on a road within the TAR has to stop at frequent checkpoints manned by armed Chinese officials. They often refuse to let Tibetan travelers pass, particularly if they are trying to enter Lhasa.

Likewise, China prohibits most Tibetans from taking advantage of the improved rail and air service. Generally, it does not permit Tibetans to leave the TAR. Despite China's proclamations, these transportation systems are not built to benefit Tibetans. They were instead designed to further China's goals in Tibet. Specifically, China wants to exploit the region's natural resources, open up its lands to Han immigrants, and dilute the influence of traditional Tibetan culture.

Forests, Minerals, and Water

Tibetans living in forested areas have long used wood as building material. Craftspeople also make wooden goods, such as printing blocks, bowls, and utensils. But without a transportation system, Tibet's lumber industry has been small. The new roads and railways are now allowing China to develop forestry in the region for the first time.

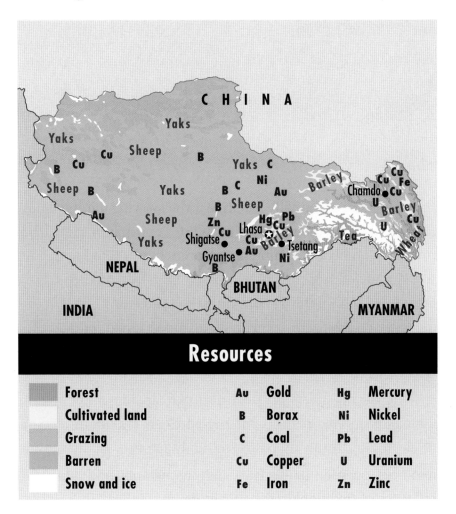

Resources

Forest	Au	Gold	Hg	Mercury
Cultivated land	B	Borax	Ni	Nickel
Grazing	C	Coal	Pb	Lead
Barren	Cu	Copper	U	Uranium
Snow and ice	Fe	Iron	Zn	Zinc

The Zangmu Dam harnesses the power of the Brahmaputra River in southern Tibet. From there, the river flows into India. Indian officials are concerned about how this and other planned Chinese dams will affect the water supply in their country.

Even more potentially lucrative is the growing mining industry. Tibet is rich with minerals, including copper, iron, gold, lead, zinc, coal, and borax. Chinese companies have started to extract these minerals, which can now easily be transported to China by rail. In 2010, mining made up only 3 percent of Tibet's gross domestic product (the total amount of goods and services produced in a year). But China projects that that number could rise to 30 percent by 2020.

The mighty rivers of Tibet also play an important role in China's economic plans. China requires an enormous amount of electricity to run its businesses and factories. By harnessing Tibet's river waters, China could produce large amounts of hydroelectric power. China is also experiencing shortages of water for use in manufacturing, mining, and farming. The country already has plans to divert the direction of Tibet's rivers to provide this needed water.

China's development of Tibet's forestry, mining, and hydroelectric industries is likely to cause environmental problems. Diverting its rivers will also threaten the local fish population and damage fertile farmland. At the same time, the economic benefits of these changes will be unlikely to go to Tibet. Instead, the Chinese government is expected to direct the income and electricity produced from the exploitation of Tibet's land to heavily populated eastern China.

What Tibet Grows, Makes, and Mines

AGRICULTURE
Barley
Wheat
Yaks

MANUFACTURING
Construction materials
Crafts
Food processing

MINING
Copper
Gold
Iron

The transportation system linking Tibet and the rest of China not only takes resources out of Tibet. It also brings Chinese people into the region. With the encouragement of the Chinese government, many Chinese, mostly of the Han ethnic group, arrive in Lhasa every day. Some come to stay. It is likely that there are now more Han Chinese living in Lhasa than there are Tibetans.

The Chinese government claims it has transformed Tibet by building modern houses, schools, and hospitals. But Tibetans argue that these are mostly for the use of the Han Chinese. Tibetans are also angry that the Han have much better access to good jobs. The vast majority of Tibet's businesses, for instance, are owned by Han rather than native Tibetans.

Some Tibetans are able to find financial success in Tibet's growing economy. But most of these people have studied in China universities outside of Tibet. Few Tibetans, however, can afford the education needed to compete in the Chinese-dominated business world of today's Tibet.

Tourism

In recent years, China has worked to revive Tibet's tourist industry. Tourism was an important part of the region's economy in the late twentieth century. At that time, most of the tourists were from North America and Europe. Many came to see the beautiful scenery or to climb mountains. Others wanted to meet monks and learn about Tibetan Buddhism firsthand.

After the protests of 2008, however, the Chinese government clamped down on foreigners entering Tibet. It did not want the outside world to know about its heavy-handed treatment of Tibetans. China now tightly controls the number of foreign tourists allowed into Tibet. Only very determined travelers with a good deal of money to spend can get in. In addition to having to obtain various permits, these tourists must hire a guide. They may only visit places specified in advance on an approved itinerary.

China, however, places no such restrictions on Chinese tourists to Tibet. With the rail lines making travel to Tibet fairly easy and affordable, vacationing Han Chinese have been flooding

into the region. The Chinese government reported in 2013 that almost thirteen million people visited Tibet, most of whom were Chinese. Eager to promote Tibetan tourism, officials have said they hope that number will rise to twenty million by 2020.

The tourist industry has created many new jobs in Tibet. But like other businesses, hotels and restaurants usually hire only Han Chinese for all but the lowest-paying positions. The growing number of Han tourists has also contributed to escalating tensions between the Tibetans and the Han Chinese.

Many Tibetans are angry that tourists overrun sacred sites such as the Jokhang Temple, where they interfere with pilgrims' prayers and rituals. These tourists generally know little about Buddhism, Tibetan culture, or the Tibetan people themselves. Han tourists, while charmed by Tibet's landmarks and awed by its scenic sites, sometimes regard Tibetans with contempt. Tibetans, in turn, view the Han in their midst with suspicion.

Tourists hire pedicab drivers in Lhasa. More than three hundred thousand people work in the tourism industry in Tibet.

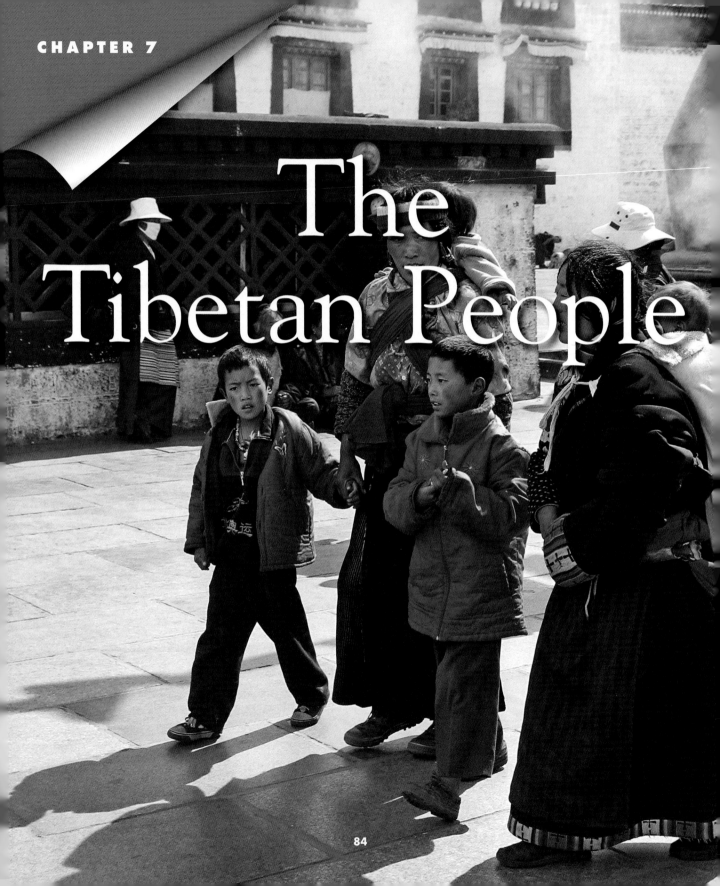

CHAPTER 7

The Tibetan People

N 2011, CHINA RELEASED INFORMATION ABOUT ITS sixth national census, conducted the year before. It said that the population of the Tibet Autonomous Region was just over 3 million, almost 15 percent larger than it had been when the previous census was taken in 2000. The 2010 census also found that about 2.7 million people, or approximately 90.5 percent, of the TAR's residents were Tibetan. About 8.2 percent were Han Chinese, and about 1.3 percent were from other ethnic groups.

Han Chinese in Tibet

Like many public pronouncements from China about Tibet, the numbers in the government's statistics are controversial. The Central Tibetan Administration, the Tibetan exile government in India, maintains that the population of Cultural Tibet, of which the TAR is just a part, is actually more than six million. They believe that Tibetans in the TAR number only about two

Ethnic Groups in Tibet*

Tibetan	90.5%
Han Chinese	8.2%
Other (including Hui, Monba, and Lhoba)	1.3%

*These figures are from the 2010 Chinese census; some Tibetans question their accuracy.

million—substantially lower than the Chinese estimate.

Many Tibetan exiles believe the number of Han stated by the Chinese government is even less accurate. They claim that so many Han Chinese have migrated to the TAR in recent years that the Han now outnumber Tibetans there. Exiles also point out that the Chinese census ignored the large number of Chinese soldiers stationed in the TAR and do not include the many Chinese officials and businesspeople who spend much of their year there.

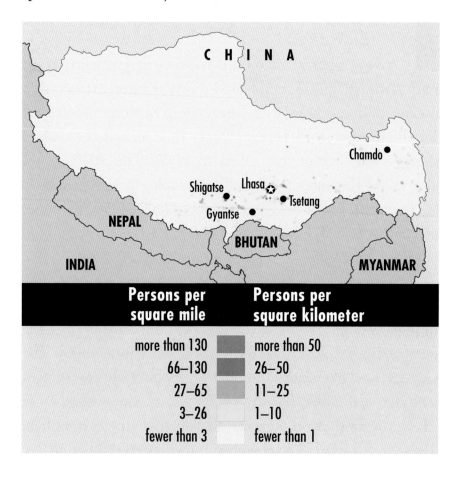

Persons per square mile		Persons per square kilometer
more than 130		more than 50
66–130		26–50
27–65		11–25
3–26		1–10
fewer than 3		fewer than 1

Rural and Urban

There have long been cities and towns in Tibet. Lhasa, for instance, has been an important urban center since the seventh century. Still, throughout most of Tibet's history, its people were largely rural. The majority of Tibetans lived in the countryside, either as settled farmers or wandering herders.

Recently, herders particularly have seen a drastic change in their way of life. The Chinese government has compelled many of them to give up their old ways. China claims that ancient herding methods are destroying Tibet's grasslands, although many ecologists do not believe this is true. More likely, China wants to remove the herders so it can have freer access to their land and the great mineral deposits beneath it.

Tibetan houses typically have flat roofs. In rural areas, blocks of yak dung, which is used as fuel, is sometimes dried on the roof.

An inscription in the
Tibetan language at a
temple in Lhasa

**Population of Largest
Cities (2010 est.)**

Lhasa	400,000
Shigatse	80,000
Chamdo	80,000
Tsetang	52,000
Gyantse	15,000

Since 2000, large numbers of Tibetan herders, especially those in Qinghai Province, have been pressured by the Chinese government to sell their animals. In exchange for giving up herding, they receive cash payments and housing in large concrete buildings constructed by the government. The Chinese government claims that it has resettled more than one million herders. It proudly touts that their new homes have indoor plumbing and electricity. The government also boasts that resettled herders now often can afford luxuries—such as color television sets and refrigerators—their grandparents or parents could never have imagined. One state-owned newspaper reported that the resettlement policies "for herders are like the warm spring breeze that brightens the grassland . . . and reaches into the herders' hearts."

But many herders are disappointed with their new lives. Some are uncomfortable in their concrete homes. Others, unable to find any paying work, are frustrated with depending on government payments for their survival. Some herders claim that the Chinese government said they would receive larger amounts of money than they actually do. Others say China promised that they could return to their lands if they wanted to, which has not proved to be the case. Some former herders merely find that they desperately miss their old way of life. In 2015, a man named Gere told a reporter, "We don't go hungry, but we have lost the life that our ancestors practiced for thousands of years."

Speaking Tibetan

Wherever they live, Tibetans share the same ethnicity and usually the same language. The majority of Tibetan speakers live in the four Chinese provinces of Xinjiang, Qinghai, Sichuan,

Writing the Tibetan Language

Tibetan did not have a written form until the seventh century. Tradition holds that King Songtsen Gampo charged a young man named Thonmi Sambhota with creating a system for writing Tibetan. The king wanted a writing system so that Buddhist texts could be translated into his language. The system Thonmi Sambhota devised was based on a script invented in India.

The form of written Tibetan used today dates from the ninth century. It includes an alphabet of thirty characters that represent consonant sounds. Vowels are indicated by diacritics, markings that appear above and below the characters. Words are written from left to right, and the syllables within them are separated by a dot.

Tibetan girls write on a blackboard in a rural school. Many nomadic children have little chance to attend school.

and Yunnan and in the TAR, where, according to the Chinese constitution, Tibetan is the official language. Large numbers of people in India, Nepal, and Bhutan also know Tibetan. In Norway, Switzerland, Taiwan, and the United States, there are sizable communities that speak Tibetan as well.

Primary school classes in the TAR are generally taught in Tibetan. But secondary schools more commonly use Mandarin

Chinese, the language spoken by the Han Chinese. Because of the large number of Han moving to the TAR in recent years, Mandarin is now often heard in the region.

Some young Tibetans learn Mandarin in school or by studying in other areas of China. Knowing Mandarin is a valuable skill. Increasingly, it is used by businesspeople and government officials in Tibet. A Mandarin-speaking Tibetan therefore has a much better chance of finding a good job.

The majority of Tibetans, however, have little opportunity to learn the language. Most young people do not attend secondary school, and very few Tibetans can afford a university education. Many Tibetans also resent the idea that they need to learn a foreign language to conduct business or just go about their daily lives in their native land. They fear that if they learn Mandarin and abandon Tibetan, they will be losing a vital part of what unites them as the Tibetan people.

Common Tibetan Words and Phrases

yin	yes
min/mé	no
trashi délek	hello
sang nyi jel yong	see you tomorrow
khyé-rang kusu dépo yin-bé?	How are you?
la yin, débo yin	I am fine
ga-lé zhu	good-bye (if leaving)
ga-lé pep	good-bye (if staying)
tuk-jé ché	thank you
lamin/tuk-jé ché	no, thank you

CHAPTER 8

Following Buddha

ABOUT 2,500 YEARS AGO, SIDDHARTHA GAUTAMA, the prince of a small kingdom in present-day Nepal, lived a life of luxury and pleasure. But leaving the palace one day, he saw an old man, a sick man, and a dead body. Witnessing such suffering led him toward a new path. He gave up his riches and lived as a poor man while devoting himself to religious searching. After many years, he abandoned this course as well, deciding instead to embrace a "middle way" between wealth and poverty.

Opposite: **A gold statue of the Buddha is one of about one hundred thousand images of the Buddha in the chorten, or dome-shaped shrine, at the Palcho Monastery in southern Tibet. It is the largest chorten in Tibet.**

Finding Enlightenment

One evening, Siddhartha Gautama sat beneath a tree. He meditated throughout the night. By dawn, he had become imbued with great spiritual knowledge. He was thereafter known as Buddha, meaning "one who is enlightened."

Buddha shared his knowledge with others. Life involved suffering, he explained. Although pleasure could relieve suffering, its effect was temporary. The cause of suffering was

Tibetan monks take part in a ceremony on Tibetan New Year.

misplaced desire. Buddha explained that through his teachings people could free themselves from worldly attachments and desire, thus ending their suffering.

The beliefs of Buddha inspired the religion of Buddhism. One of the major religions of the world, it has approximately 376 million followers. Nearly all Tibetans are Buddhists. Large numbers of Buddhists are also found in nearby Nepal, India, Bhutan, Mongolia, and parts of Russia. Many East Asian countries, such as Cambodia and Thailand, are predominantly Buddhist. And increasingly, people in North America, Europe, and Australia are also embracing spiritual practices associated with Buddhism.

Buddhism and Bon

Buddhism as practiced in Tibet was strongly influenced by Indian scholars, who introduced the religion to the region in

the seventh century. Tibetan Buddhism also includes elements of older traditions, which eventually became known as the Bon religion. In the Bon religion, priests perform rituals to win the favor of various gods and spirits and to ensure that the dead will fare well in the afterlife. The rituals often involve making offerings of food or drink or sacrificing horses, yaks, or other animals to please the gods.

After Buddhism became the state religion of Tibet, the authorities did not try to discourage belief in the older Bon gods. Instead, these gods were incorporated into the practice of Tibetan Buddhism. The Indian scholar Padmasambhava, who came to Tibet's royal court in the eighth century, is still revered for taming the gods and transforming them into guardians, rather than enemies, of Buddhism. Today, belief in supernatural beings still plays an important role in the daily lives of most Tibetans. Through a combination of old rituals and Buddhist practices, they try to pacify dangerous spirits that otherwise might do them harm.

Tibetans pray outside the Jokhang Temple in Lhasa, the most revered religious building in the region.

Over time, various schools of Buddhism developed in Tibet. The oldest is Nyingma. It is said to have been founded by Padmasambhava. In the eleventh century, the Kagyu and Sakya schools were introduced. Three centuries later, Tsongkhapa Lozang Drakpa established the Geluk, or "Virtuous School." Now the most prominent school of Tibetan Buddhism, it counts the Dalai Lama among its followers. The differences in the beliefs held by these groups are relatively minor. Although temples are generally devoted to one school, Tibetans feel free to worship in whatever temple they prefer, regardless of its affiliation.

Precious Teacher

When the Tibetan king Trisong Detsen wanted to build a great Buddhist monastery, he faced resistance from his court. A Buddhist temple had been destroyed by floodwaters. The royal residence at Lhasa was struck by lightning. The court took these events as signs that the local gods were not pleased by the king's interest in Buddhism.

To ease their concerns, the king invited Padmasambhava to Lhasa. From the Swat Valley of what is now Pakistan, Padmasambhava was well known for his ability to tame angry gods. According to old Tibetan stories, he called out the names of the gods who were making trouble in Tibet, and they came to him in human form. He taught them about Buddhism and calmed their fury. The court, however, still disliked Padmasambhava and spread rumors that he wanted to overthrow the king, who became suspicious of the holy man. Padmasambhava escaped from Lhasa, even though the court sent archers to kill him. Using his powers, Padmasambhava froze the assassins in place and got away.

For many centuries, Padmasambhava has been celebrated by the people of Tibet. There he is also known as Guru Rinpoche, or Precious Teacher. Padmasambhava is now considered the founder of Nyingma, one of four schools of Buddhism practiced in Tibet.

Death and Rebirth

Central to the beliefs of Tibetan Buddhists is the idea of karma. According to this idea, all good or bad things that happen to a person are related to their behavior in a previous life. Past cruel and unkind actions are the cause of present-day miseries, while past generosity and compassion result in present-day good fortune. Buddhists are also concerned about the good or bad karma they collect during their lifetime because it determines who or what they will become after death.

Tibetan Buddhist monks dress in red robes.

When they die, Buddhists expect to be reincarnated, or born again by their souls entering other beings. These beings reside in six different realms. Those who have accumulated good karma in their previous existence might be reincarnated in the realm of the gods. There, they will live a long and happy life. But the best realm in which to be reborn is the human realm. As a human, a being has the best chance of achieving enlightenment, like Buddha. Enlightenment is the goal of every Tibetan Buddhist. Only enlightenment can end the constant cycle of birth, death, and rebirth.

A life full of bad karma might lead to rebirth in the realm of the angry gods, who are warlike beings full of hate. Another dreaded fate is being sent to the realm of the hungry ghosts, whose unsatisfied desires keep them attached to the realm of humans. Being reborn in the animal world is also bad, because animals do not have the awareness to become enlightened. The worst place to be reincarnated is the realm of hell. There, souls are tortured until their bad karma is erased.

A person's next life is also said to be influenced by his or her experience in the bardo, the period between death and rebirth. During the forty-nine days of the bardo, a lama prays and performs rituals to help the dead move from their old body into their new one. Loved ones can also help the deceased through meditation and other spiritual practices. Aiding others in the bardo allows people to prepare for their own death and their future experience there.

Mantras

The daily practice of Tibetan Buddhism also involves repeating mantras. Mantras are sacred sayings, sometimes made up of just a single word or syllable. To keep track of how many times they have said a mantra, worshipers often use strings of prayer beads made of wood, bone, or coral. By tradition, these strings include 108 beads, which is considered a sacred number. Each time people say a mantra, they move a bead until they have gone through the entire string. Usually one or two strings with smaller beads are attached. These are used to

record each time the worshiper has said a complete round of 108 mantras.

In addition to saying mantras, Tibetans hoist strings of player flags on poles and rooftops. Written on the flags are prayers. Each time a flag flutters in the wind, the prayer is sent out into the universe.

Prayer wheels provide an even more efficient way of repeating prayers. A small prayer wheel is made up of a metal cylinder, about 2 inches (5 cm) high, attached to a handle. Inside the cylinder is a scroll on which a prayer is written. By hand or by use of a weight, the worshiper spins the cylinder around. Each rotation sends out a prayer.

Temples and monasteries house giant prayer wheels. The largest have cylinders measuring about 9 feet (2.7 m) high and scrolls with a prayer printed thousands of times. The biggest prayer wheels need waterpower to move the cylinder and release its prayers.

Monuments, Monasteries, and Temples

Buddhism influences every aspect of Tibetans' daily lives. Visible everywhere in the country are symbols of their faith—from prayer flags to temples to statues of Buddha. For instance, religious monuments called chortens (also known as stupas) are found throughout Tibet. Each chorten has a mound-shaped base topped by a steeple-like structure. These monuments honor Buddha and other religious figures. They often contain bodily remains or sacred objects.

Everything about a chorten is symbolic. For example, its square base represents the earth, while the steps symbolize fire.

A shrine in a Tibetan home typically includes images of the Buddha and an incense burner.

Before the Chinese invasion of Tibet, just about every town or village was home to a monastery. There, lamas taught young monks about Buddhist texts and rituals. At least one child from each family was expected to join a religious order. In 1950, an estimated one-fourth of the Tibetan population was part a monastic community.

Most of Tibet's monasteries were destroyed during the Cultural Revolution of the 1960s and 1970s. But those that have since been rebuilt and reopened remain important to the religious life of the Tibetan people. The monks they train perform ceremonies and rituals at Buddhist temples.

Tibetan Buddhists do not have to go to temples to worship, however. Many people make religious offerings at shrines in their homes. Household shrines usually consist of a few candles, an incense burner, and a small statue of Buddha.

Jokhang Temple

The most sacred building in Tibet is the Jokhang Temple, which lies in the oldest section of Lhasa. Known for its red exterior and gold roof, it is the most popular tourist site in Tibet. It is also visited by Buddhist pilgrims from around the world. Before entering it, people often stop and pray. The air outside is always full of the sound of mantras and the smell of yak butter and juniper branches, which Tibetans burn as a religious offering. Near the temple is a bustling outdoor market that serves both pilgrims and tourists. Its stalls sell everything from prayer flags to cowboy hats.

The four-story temple complex includes numerous dimly lit shrines. Surrounding it are three circumambulation routes, paths that circle around sacred shrines and temples. The faithful go on these routes a number of times. In the Tibetan language, this type of ritual behavior is called a *kora*. During a kora, a Buddhist walks

around a sacred site, always in a clockwise direction, while chanting mantras and spinning prayer wheels.

Jokhang Temple was originally built in 639 by King Songtsen Gampo. One of his wives, Princess Wencheng, had a vision of a huge female demon sleeping below the ground of Tibet. King Songtsen Gampo ordered twelve temples built to anchor the demon's body, so she would be unable to rise out of the earth. The Jokhang Temple sits directly over where the demon's heart is supposed to lie. It now houses the Jowo Sakyamuni statue that Princess Wencheng presented to her husband after their marriage. The most revered statue in Tibet, it is said to have been blessed by Buddha himself.

CHAPTER 9

Art, Music, and Sports

FOR MANY CENTURIES, ART AND MUSIC HAVE BEEN AT the center of the practice of Tibetan Buddhism. Paintings, sculptures, songs, and dance all play an important role in rituals and ceremonies. Painted images are also tools for meditation. Tibetan Buddhists concentrate on these images to help them achieve greater spiritual understanding.

Religious Art

Monks and other artisans create paintings on the walls of temples and monasteries. They also make paintings on cloth called *thangkas*. Thangkas are displayed as banners during religious rituals and hung in temples and homes. A bamboo rod is attached to the bottom of a thangka. By rolling up a thangka like a scroll around the bamboo, it can be transported easily from place to place.

Tibet has a long history of intricate metalwork.

Many thangkas depict Buddha, gods, and lamas. But these images are not meant to tell a story, like many Christian religious paintings are. They are instead intended to help people reach a spiritual state. In depicting the figures on a thangka, artisans have to follow a strict code. For example, in images of Buddha, his features have to be shown in a very specific way. Even the distance between his eyes and the width of his ears have to be measured precisely.

Some thangkas depict mandalas. Mandalas are diagrams of the universe. They usually picture a circle with circles, squares, and triangles inside it. The image is always symmetrical, meaning the left side mirrors the right side, because Tibetan Buddhists believe the universe is in perfect order and harmony.

Tibetan artisans are also skilled in metalworking. They create ornaments and religious objects from bronze, silver, and other metals. Temples, monasteries, and household shrines feature statues of Buddha and other religious figures, which are crafted from metal, stone, or ivory. Some of the most impressive religious statues in Tibet stand several stories high.

Opera

Tibet's most popular performing art is opera. The style called *lhamo* is said to have been created by the Buddhist lama Thangtong Gyalpo in the fourteenth century. He taught seven sisters to sing and dance as he played percussion instruments. Early audiences said the sisters sang like goddesses, the literal meaning of the word *lhamo*. Ever since then, traveling troups of lhamo singers and dancers have performed at festivals and ceremonies.

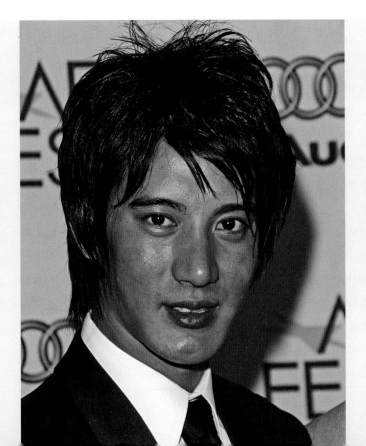

A Tibetan Star

A beautiful voice and leading-man looks have made Purba Rgyal a star in China's entertainment industry. An ethnic Tibetan, he was born in Sichuan Province in 1985. After studying acting at the Shanghai Theatre Academy, he became the winning contestant on *My Hero*, a televised singing competition. In 2008, he released his first album titled *Love Is So Simple*. Purba Rgyal now frequently appears in movies and on television. His most famous film is *Prince of the Himalayas* (2006), in which he played the title role. The movie is an adaptation of William Shakespeare's play *Hamlet*, set in ancient Tibet.

Performers in Tibetan opera often wear masks.

Each performance begins with an offering to the gods. Then, speaking quickly and in a high pitch, a narrator describes the plot. He also introduces the characters as they appear onstage. The players wear colorful clothes and walk in a distinctive way to indicate whether their characters are good or evil. The performers speak dialogue, sing, and dance, accompanied by a chorus of six women and musicians playing drums and cymbals.

Traditionally, a lhamo took place over several days, though today they usually last only a few hours. There are ten classical lhamo dramas depicting myths and historical events, but players sometimes create new ones. In the exile community in India, for instance, lhamo companies perform political operas that call for Tibet's independence from China. In the Tibet Autonomous Region, the lhamo has also changed with the times by adopting certain Chinese theatrical styles.

Preserving Culture

In 1959, the Dalai Lama and tens of thousands of Tibetans fled to India. As the exiles began to build a community in the town of Dharamsala, one of the first things the Dalai Lama did was establish the Tibetan Institute of Performing Arts (TIPA). The institute was meant to preserve Tibetan culture, particularly the form of opera known as lhamo. TIPA now employs a permanent company of more than fifty singers and dancers. The company performs during traditional ceremonies. It also travels to Tibetan exile settlements throughout the world to share this time-honored musical art form.

Literature

Because of the importance of Buddhism in everyday life, much of Tibet's literature consists of religious writings. In the seventh century, written Tibetan was invented to record events at court, keep accounts, and translate ancient texts. By the end of the eleventh century, Tibetans began translating Buddhist texts en masse. More than five thousand Buddhist texts were translated into Tibetan between the eighth and the seventeenth centuries. They are divided into the Kangyur and the Tengyur. The Kangyur were texts based on teachings communicated by Buddha. The Tengyur were works attributed to Indian religious scholars. Tibetans also wrote their own Buddhist histories, biographies, and poetry. One famous story is of a Buddhist saint named Milarepa, who overcame great hardship in his life and attained enlightenment.

Tibetans also wrote down legends and stories that had been passed down by word of mouth. The most important of these was *The Epic of King Gesar*. Written in the eleventh century, it tells the story of a leader with magical powers who ruled the mythical kingdom of Ling. Another famous work of Tibetan literature is *The Tale of the Incomparable Prince*. Written by Tsering Wanggyel in the eighteenth century, it is considered the first Tibetan novel. After surviving the schemes of evil members of the court, the prince of the title brings teachers of Buddhism to his kingdom.

A young Tibetan woman reads a book.

Modern Tibetan literature consists of works written both by Tibetans living within China and by Tibetans in exile around the globe. In China, Tibetan authors face restrictions on what they can write about, because government officials can ban their works. People in Tibet tend to have little knowledge of the writings of Tibetan exiles, which are not allowed into China, but this is changing as more Tibetans have access to social media. Dorje Tsering Chenaktsang, who writes under the name Jangbu, is often considered the greatest living Tibetan poet. A longtime editor of a literary journal in Lhasa, he is now a professor in Paris, France. His works include *The Nine-Eyed Agate* (2010), a mix of poetry and short stories that offers a vivid look at modern Tibet.

Most exiled Tibetan writers are highly critical of China. Among them are Jamyang Norbu, a political activist who writes essays and novels in English and Tibetan. Poet and essayist Tenzin Tsundue is also well known for his involvement in the Tibetan independence movement.

Tenzin Tsundue takes part in a protest for Tibetan independence in New York City. Tsundue, who grew up in India, is the son of Tibetans who were forced to leave Tibet.

Writing Without Fear

Because of her courageous criticism of the Chinese government, Tsering Woeser is a hero to many young Tibetans. Born in Lhasa in 1966, she studied Chinese literature in Sichuan Province, where she later worked as a magazine editor. After publishing a collection of poems, Woeser wrote a book of short stories and prose called *Notes on Tibet* (2003). Written in Mandarin Chinese, it became a best seller. It also upset the Chinese government, because in the book Woeser was critical of China's treatment of the Tibetan people. Her writing has since been banned in mainland China. But by writing about Tibet on the Internet, she has continued to reach many Tibetan and Han Chinese readers.

In 2013, the U.S. government honored Woeser with the International Women of Courage Award. However, she was unable to attend the award ceremony in Washington, D.C., because the Chinese government would not allow her to leave the country.

Sports

Many Tibetans still enjoy the traditional sports that their ancestors played centuries ago. Herding families, for instance, come together at yearly festivals to watch horse races. Riders also compete in tests of horsemanship. In one competition, *khatak*, or white scarves, are placed on the racing track. Each rider tries to pick up the khatak while galloping by on horseback. The rider with the most scarves at the end of the game wins. In another contest, riders shoot guns at targets while their horses gallop at full speed.

In some parts of Tibet, yak racing is also popular. Riders

dress both themselves and their yaks in colorful garb. Scarves and ribbons adorn the animals' fur and horns.

Other traditional Tibetan sports include archery, wrestling, and tug-of-war. But perhaps the most unusual game played in Tibet is stone carrying. As a show of strength, men hoist heavy boulders weighing as much as 300 pounds (135 kg) onto their shoulders and carry them around a circular track. To make the feat more challenging, the stones are covered with butter before the competition, making them even harder to hold on to.

Yak racing is a popular part of many Tibetan festivals. Yaks can run quickly, but only for short distances, so they sometimes slow to a walk by the time they reach the finish line.

An Olympic Champion

Growing up in a Tibetan family of herders in the Chinese province of Qinghai, Choeyang Kyi had always loved running through the countryside. Her athletic skill won her a place on the Chinese team that traveled to London, England, for the 2012 Summer Olympics. That year, twenty-one-year-old Choeyang Kyi, known as Qieyang Shenjie in China, became the first person of Tibetan ancestry to compete in any Olympic game.

In the women's 20-kilometer walk, Choeyang Kyi came in third, winning a bronze medal. Her Olympic win did not come without controversy, however. Many Tibetans around the world celebrated her victory. But others were upset that, because of China's political domination over Tibet, Choeyang Kyi had represented China rather than Tibet, which has never had its own Olympic team. Dickyi Choeyang, the spokesperson for the Tibetan exile government in India, said, "[a]s an individual, we wish her well; she must have put in a lot of effort to reach there. But we are sad that she cannot represent a free Tibet."

Choeyang Kyi tried her best to steer clear of the controversy, often refusing to answer reporters' questions. She was perhaps leery of saying anything that might offend the Chinese authorities, who declared that her achievements were proof that Tibetans were

thriving under China's rule. But when she was asked about cheering fans in London waving the Tibetan flag, which is now forbidden in China, she could not contain her glee for their support. "I heard it!" Choeyang Kyi blurted out. "I heard a Tibetan cheering me on!"

Soccer is the favorite modern sport of Tibetans living within China. It is also popular with the Tibetan exile community in India. There, the biggest sporting event each year is the Gyelyum Chenmo Memorial Gold Cup tournament, which is named in honor of the Dalai Lama's mother. In 2015, teams of

Tibetans from India, the United States, Canada, Nepal, and several European nations competed.

Tibetan monks play soccer in a monastery courtyard.

The exiles in India have also established their own national team. However, they are not allowed to compete in the World Cup, the leading international soccer tournament, because Tibet is not recognized as a country separate from China. Instead, they can play foreign teams under the organization of the New Federation Board. Established in 2003, it represents teams from peoples who, like the Tibetan exiles, are seeking political independence but do not yet have their own country.

CHAPTER 10

Tibetan Life

EVERYDAY LIFE IN TIBET IS A MIX OF THE OLD AND THE new. Under the rule of the Chinese government, Tibetans have been forced to give up some of the customs of their ancestors and adopt the ways of modern Chinese life. Despite this pressure, Tibetans still maintain many of their old traditions—from the food they eat to the clothes they wear to the festivals and celebrations they enjoy together.

Tsampa and Yak Butter

The cuisine of Tibet is largely limited by what plants can grow and what animals can live at a high elevation. The staple food of Tibet is a type of barley that can thrive in Tibetan farms. *Tsampa,* or toasted barley flour, is particularly popular, especially when mixed with sugar, butter, or milk in a dish called *pak.* Other grains grown in Tibet include millet, oats,

and wheat. From wheat flour, Tibetans make noodles and dough. Cooks often fill dough with meat to create *momos*, or steamed dumplings. They steam or fry dough to prepare bread. They also use buckwheat to make pancakes.

Dairy products are another important part of the Tibetan diet. From the milk of *dri*, female yaks, they make butter, cream, and yogurt. Other sources of milk are cows and *dzos*, animals that are a cross between a cow and a yak.

In southern Tibet, where farms are located, Tibetans primarily eat vegetables, grains, and milk. To the north, though, nomads of the plateau usually need to eat meat to survive. According to the Buddhist religion, they show respect to the animals they slaughter. To take as few animal lives as possible, Tibetans prefer to kill one large animal for meat instead of several small ones.

The most popular beverage in Tibet is tea, which is mostly imported from other parts of China. Tea is often mixed with butter, cream, and salt to make a thick, hearty brew. Today, some younger and less traditional Tibetans prefer sweet tea to salty butter tea. Tibetans also drink *chang*, a type of beer made from barley.

Butter Tea

Butter tea is the most popular beverage in Tibet. Tibetans especially enjoy drinking the hot tea on days when the weather is cold. The tea is not only warming, but also filling, because it is made with dri milk and dri butter. This simple version of Tibetan butter tea uses cow's milk instead. Have an adult help you with this recipe.

Ingredients

2 cups water

1 tea bag of black or Darjeeling tea

Salt

¼ cup whole milk

1 tablespoon unsalted butter

Directions

1. Boil the water in a small saucepan.
2. Turn off the heat and place the tea bag in the pan. Let it steep for about two minutes.
3. Remove the tea bag. Add a large pinch of salt and the milk to the tea.
4. Add the butter to the tea. Stir the tea quickly with a whisk or a fork until the butter is completely melted.
5. Pour the tea into two mugs and share your butter tea with a friend.

Music and dancing are part of most Tibetan wedding celebrations.

Marrying in Tibet

Before the mid-twentieth century, it was not uncommon for a woman to have several husbands or a man to have several wives. Particularly in rural areas, these marital arrangements were practical. For instance, several brothers might marry the same woman to preserve the family's plot of land. If the brothers each had their own wife and family, the land would have to be split up between them when their father died. But if they shared a wife, the plot would remain intact. A large plot was more productive and profitable than smaller ones, so everyone in the family would benefit.

Under Chinese rule, however, these marriage practices were outlawed. But some Tibetans, especially those in the countryside, still have group marriages. In urban areas, though, marriages almost always involve just one man and one woman.

Sky Burials

Tibetan Buddhists believe that after death a person is reborn. The body the deceased leaves behind is seen as nothing but an empty shell. Rather than burying the remains in the earth, relatives have the corpse cut up and allow it to be fed to vultures. Known as a sky burial, this practice is consistent with Buddhist beliefs about feeling compassion for all living things. The offering of human flesh not only provides food for the vultures, but also saves the lives of the animals the vultures would eat otherwise.

In the past, parents usually arranged their children's marriages. But now couples often meet at social gatherings, and then ask for their parents' permission to marry. Families consult a lama and an astrologer to make sure the couple is compatible. Astrologers also determine the best day for the bride and groom to marry. The wedding, held at the home of the groom's family, is followed by a great feast.

Living Together

Households are usually made up of parents and their unmarried children. As the parents grow older, their children take on more family responsibilities, allowing the parents to spend more time on religious activities. They believe this will help them fare well in their next life.

The type of house a family has depends on where they live. Houses in southern Tibet are typically flat-roofed dwellings made of stone or clay. In forested areas, wooden houses are common. The walls of Tibetan houses slope slightly inward.

Stealing Horses for Fun

Horse Thief is an old Tibetan children's game. The players organize into two teams, with each team standing in a line facing the other team. A player on one team is the "buyer." A player on the other is the "seller." The rest of the players on both teams are "horses." They are supposed to whinny and neigh while the game is played.

The buyer approaches the seller and tries to make a deal for one of the "horses" on the seller's team. While they negotiate, the buyer will suddenly tap a horse to try to "steal" it. The buyer then runs back to his team's line. If he gets back without being tapped by the stolen horse, the horse has to join the buyer's team. The two teams take turns until one team has stolen all the other's horses.

This construction technique helps keep them from collapsing during an earthquake.

Traditionally, nomadic herders in the north lived in animal-skin or canvas tents. They could easily pack up the tents and move them as they traveled with their animals. Some herder families still spend part of the year in tents. But many recently

Tibetan children playing at a monastery

This man is wearing only one sleeve of his chuba, which is commonly done in warmer weather.

have moved into concrete housing built by the Chinese government. Families in Lhasa also are likely to live in newly constructed apartment buildings made of concrete and steel.

Chubas and Jewelry

In Tibet, it is often hot during the day and cold during the night. A traditional Tibetan robe called a chuba is an ideal garment for dealing with such fluctuating temperatures. Both men and women wear chubas. Hanging below the knees, chubas are held in place with a sash at the waist. A chuba's sleeves are very long, sometimes extending a foot below the fingers. In cold weather, the sleeves keep the wearer's hands warm. In hot weather, the sleeves can be rolled up easily. Similarly, during the day, people stay cool by hiking up their chubas to expose their legs or by taking off the upper portion and tying the garment around their waist by the sleeves.

Traditional Tibetan headdresses often feature colorful stones.

In the chilly north, chubas are usually made of sheepskin, with the wool side worn toward the body. These warm cloaks can double as blankets on cold nights. In the warmer south, chubas are often sewn from woolen cloth.

In urban areas, especially in Lhasa, many people no longer wear chubas. They instead dress in modern Chinese clothing. Many Tibetans in exile, however, make a point of wearing traditional clothes. They want to preserve all aspects of Tibetan culture, including clothing styles.

Jewelry has long played an important role in Tibetan society. Before the Chinese invasion of 1950, the small number of wealthy Tibetans wore expensive jewelry to show off their high status. But even the poorest Tibetans usually owned a few ornaments. Both men and women wore necklaces, earrings, and a *gau*, a small box that holds amulets, objects that are supposed to protect people from harm. Women also wore headdresses, which they often inherited from their mothers when they got married. Headdresses were decorated with pearls, turquoise, and coral.

In the 1920s, the thirteenth Dalai Lama outlawed expensive jewelry. He was upset that poorer families were spending so much of their money on it. The Chinese also frowned on the Tibetan practice of wearing ornaments. During antireligious campaigns between 1956 and 1976, soldiers stole and destroyed many pieces of Tibetan jewelry, which was often the only thing of value that families owned. Restrictions on jewelry have since been relaxed, so many Tibetans today still wear traditional jewelry as they go about their daily chores. Headdresses, however, are rarely seen except at special occasions, such as weddings or festivals.

Celebrating Tibet

In Tibet, public holidays mandated by the Chinese government are observed throughout the year. On these holidays, government offices and some businesses close. But to Tibetans, these celebrations are not particularly important. One controversial holiday is Serf Emancipation Day, which commemorates the day that China dissolved the Tibetan government after the 1959 uprising. Tibetans do not see this as an event worthy of celebration. From their perspective, the holiday instead is a grim reminder of the decades of oppression they have endured under Chinese rule.

Public Holidays in Tibet

New Year's Day	January 1
Chinese New Year	February
Serf Emancipation Day	March 28
Tomb-Sweeping Day	April 4 to 5
Labor Day	May 1 to 3
Dragon Boat Festival	May or June
Mid-Autumn Festival	September or October
National Day	October 1 to 7

Tibetans, however, are enthusiastic about celebrating their many traditional festivals. These festivals are generally related to the practice of Buddhism. The Saga Dawa Festival, for instance, commemorates the birth and enlightenment of Buddha. The Ganden Ngachö Festival honors Tsongkhapa Lozang Drakpa, a great scholar of Tibetan Buddhism. During this celebration, Tibetans place burning lamps filled with butter on the roofs and windowsills of their houses. For the Shoton Festival, Tibetans gather at Norbulingka, the former summer home of the Dalai Lama, to watch traditional Tibetan operas.

The month-long Lingka Festival is particularly important for the nomadic herders. Wearing traditional dress, they come together to celebrate the beginning of spring. The festival also commemorates Padmasambhava, the religious leader who was said to have driven evil forces out of Tibet so that Buddhism could thrive there.

The most elaborate festival comes at the beginning of the Tibetan year. Losar is held on the first day of the Tibetan calendar, which usually falls in February. During this New Year celebration, Tibetans make offerings at temples, stupas, and household shrines. They also eat special foods, including fried cookies called *khapse*. After visiting with family and friends, celebrants wash their bodies and put on new clothes to greet the new year.

Throughout Losar, Tibetans pray for the well-being of their people and their nation. For decades, the survival of both have been under continual threat by Chinese authorities. But whether living in China, India, or far-flung countries around the globe, Tibetans everywhere still hold on to the same dream for the future: to one day live peacefully and free in their beloved homeland.

Butter lamps line the walls of Jokhang Temple during the Ganden Ngachö Festival. These lamps traditionally burned yak butter, but now other fuels are often used.

Timeline

<table>
<tr><th>TIBETAN HISTORY</th><th></th><th>WORLD HISTORY</th><th></th></tr>
<tr><td></td><td></td><td>ca. 2500 BCE</td><td>The Egyptians build the pyramids and the Sphinx in Giza.</td></tr>
<tr><td></td><td></td><td>ca. 563 BCE</td><td>The Buddha is born in India.</td></tr>
<tr><td>Legendary figure Nyatri Tsenpo becomes the first king of Tibet.</td><td>127 BCE</td><td></td><td></td></tr>
<tr><td></td><td></td><td>313 CE</td><td>The Roman emperor Constantine legalizes Christianity.</td></tr>
<tr><td>Songtsen Gampo unifies Tibet and establishes the first Buddhist temples there.</td><td>600s CE</td><td>610</td><td>The Prophet Muhammad begins preaching a new religion called Islam.</td></tr>
<tr><td>Tibet briefly takes control of the Chinese capital of Chang'an (now Xi'an).</td><td>700s</td><td></td><td></td></tr>
<tr><td>The Tibetan kingdom disbands after the assassination of King Lang Darma.</td><td>840s</td><td></td><td></td></tr>
<tr><td></td><td></td><td>1054</td><td>The Eastern (Orthodox) and Western (Roman Catholic) Churches break apart.</td></tr>
<tr><td></td><td></td><td>1095</td><td>The Crusades begin.</td></tr>
<tr><td>Mongol forces invade Tibet.</td><td>1240</td><td>1215</td><td>King John seals the Magna Carta.</td></tr>
<tr><td></td><td></td><td>1300s</td><td>The Renaissance begins in Italy.</td></tr>
<tr><td></td><td></td><td>1347</td><td>The plague sweeps through Europe.</td></tr>
<tr><td></td><td></td><td>1453</td><td>Ottoman Turks capture Constantinople, conquering the Byzantine Empire.</td></tr>
<tr><td></td><td></td><td>1492</td><td>Columbus arrives in North America.</td></tr>
<tr><td></td><td></td><td>1500s</td><td>Reformers break away from the Catholic Church, and Protestantism is born.</td></tr>
<tr><td>Ngawang Lozang Gyatso, the fifth Dalai Lama, builds the Potala Palace.</td><td>1600s</td><td>1776</td><td>The U.S. Declaration of Independence is signed.</td></tr>
<tr><td></td><td></td><td>1789</td><td>The French Revolution begins.</td></tr>
<tr><td></td><td></td><td>1865</td><td>The American Civil War ends.</td></tr>
<tr><td></td><td></td><td>1879</td><td>The first practical lightbulb is invented.</td></tr>
</table>

TIBETAN HISTORY

British soldiers enter Tibet; Tibetan leaders sign a trade agreement.	**1904**
Chinese troops invade Tibet.	**1910**
Tibet declares its political independence.	**1913**
Chinese troops enter Tibet.	**1950**
China gains control over Tibet with the Seventeen Point Agreement.	**1951**
The Dalai Lama escapes to India and establishes the Tibetan government in exile.	**1959**
China establishes the Tibet Autonomous Region (TAR).	**1965**
Most Tibetan monasteries are destroyed during China's Cultural Revolution.	**1960s–1970s**
The Dalai Lama is awarded the Nobel Peace Prize.	**1989**
The eleventh Panchen Lama is detained by Chinese authorities and disappears.	**1995**
A railway connecting Beijing in China and Lhasa in Tibet is completed.	**2006**
The Dalai Lama transfers his political responsibilities to Sikyong Lobsang Sangay.	**2011**
Tibetans around the world celebrate the Dalai Lama's eightieth birthday.	**2015**

WORLD HISTORY

1914	World War I begins.
1917	The Bolshevik Revolution brings communism to Russia.
1929	A worldwide economic depression begins.
1939	World War II begins.
1945	World War II ends.
1969	Humans land on the Moon.
1975	The Vietnam War ends.
1989	The Berlin Wall is torn down as communism crumbles in Eastern Europe.
1991	The Soviet Union breaks into separate states.
2001	Terrorists attack the World Trade Center in New York City and the Pentagon near Washington, D.C.
2004	A tsunami in the Indian Ocean destroys coastlines in Africa, India, and Southeast Asia.
2008	The United States elects its first African American president.

Fast Facts

Official name: Tibet Autonomous Region (province-level administrative area within the People's Republic of China)

Capital: Lhasa

Official language: Tibetan

Lhasa

Tibetan flag

Official religion:	None
Year of founding:	1965
National anthem (of China):	"Yiyongjun Jinxingqu" ("The March of the Volunteers")
Government:	Communist state
Head of state (of China):	President
Head of government (of China):	Premier
Head of Tibet Autonomous Region:	Chairman
Head of Tibetan government in exile:	Sikyong
Area:	471,662 square miles (1,221,600 sq km)
Bordering countries:	India, Nepal, Bhutan, and Myanmar to the south; the Chinese provinces of Qinghai, Sichuan, and Yunnan lie to the east; the Xinjiang Uyghur Autonomous Region, also part of China, is to the north
Highest elevation:	Mount Everest (called Jomolungma in Tibet), 29,035 feet (8,850 m) above sea level
Average high temperature:	June, 82°F (28°C)
Average annual rainfall:	5 to 15 inches (13 to 38 cm)

Mount Everest

Namtso Lake

Currency

Tibetan population (2014 est.): 3,180,000

Population of largest cities (2010 est.):

Lhasa	400,000
Shigatse	80,000
Chamdo	80,000
Tsetang	52,000
Gyantse	15,000

Landmarks:
- ▶ *Jokhang Temple,* Lhasa
- ▶ *Namtso Lake*
- ▶ *Potala Palace,* Lhasa
- ▶ *Qomolangma National Park,* Mount Everest
- ▶ *Tashilhunpo Monastery,* Shigatse

Economy: Traditionally, most Tibetans were employed in farming and animal herding. In recent years, China has spent billions to modernize Tibet's economy, primarily by investing money in constructing buildings, roads, and rail systems. China also has plans to develop Tibet's forestry and mining industries. Tourism, mostly by Han Chinese, is similarly likely to play an important role in Tibet's economic future.

Currency: The yuan. In 2016, 1 Chinese yuan equaled US$0.15 and US$1 was worth 6.5 Chinese yuan.

System of weights and measures: Metric system

Literacy rate (2010): China, 96%; TAR, 62%

Schoolchildren

Tsering Woeser

Common Tibetan words and phrases:

yin	yes
min/mé	no
trashi délek	hello
sang nyi jel yong	see you tomorrow
khyé-rang kusu dépo yin-bé?	How are you?
la yin, débo yin	I am fine
ga-lé zhu	good-bye (if leaving)
ga-lé pep	good-bye (if staying)
tuk-jé ché	thank you

Prominent Tibetans:

Choeyang Kyi   (1990–)
Olympic athlete

Dorje Tsering Chenaktsang (Jangbu)   (1963–)
Poet

Lobsang Sangay   (1968–)
Political leader of the Central Tibetan Administration

Songtsen Gampo   (ca. 605–ca. 649)
King of Tibet

Tenzin Gyatso   (1935–)
The fourteenth Dalai Lama

Tsering Woeser   (1966–)
Essayist and poet

To Find Out More

Books

► Harris, Joseph. *Tibet*. New York: Benchmark Books, 2010.

► Hyde-Chambers, Frederick, and Audrey Hyde-Chambers. *Tibetan Folk Tales*. Boulder, CO: Shambhala, 2001.

► Sullivan, Anne Marie. *Dalai Lama: Spiritual Leader of Tibet*. Broomhall, PA: Mason Crest, 2014.

► Thompson, Mel. *Buddhism*. Vancouver, BC: Whitecap Books, 2010.

DVDs

► *The Lost World of Tibet*. London: BBC, 2007.

► *The Sun Behind the Clouds*. New York: Zeitgeist Films, 2010.

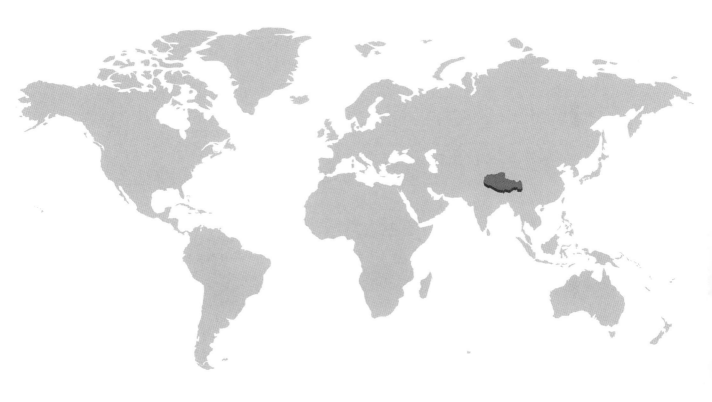

▶ Visit this Scholastic Web site for more information on Tibet:

www.factsfornow.scholastic.com

Enter the keyword Tibet

Index

Page numbers in *italics*
indicate illustrations.

Meet the Author

LIZ SONNEBORN, A GRADUATE OF Swarthmore College, lives in Brooklyn, New York. She has written more than one hundred books for adults and young readers, specializing in American and world history and biography. Her books include *Harriet Beecher Stowe* (2009), *The Great Black Migrations* (2010), *The American Indian Experience* (2010), *Ancient China* (2013), and *A to Z of American Women in the Performing Arts, Revised Edition* (2016). Sonneborn is also the author of numerous volumes for the Enchantment of the World Series, including *Canada, Iraq, North Korea, Pakistan,* and *France.*

Photo Credits

Photographs ©:

cover: dibrova/Shutterstock, Inc.; back cover: Yan Liao/age fotostock; 2: Henry Westheim Photography/Alamy Images; 5: Dennis Walton/Getty Images; 6 left: Feng Wei Photography/Getty Images; 6 center: Dennis Cox/Alamy Images; 6 right: Leisa Tyler/Getty Images; 7 left: John Lander/Alamy Images; 7 right: Boaz Rottem/Superstock, Inc.; 8: robertharding/Superstock, Inc.; 10: Everett Collection/Superstock, Inc.; 11: TopFoto/The Image Works; 13: Kammerer/ullstein bild/The Image Works; 14: Allen Berezovsky/Getty Images; 15: Zoonar GmbH/Alamy Images; 16: Daniel Berehulak/Getty Images; 18: Panorama Images/The Image Works; 21 top: Feng Wei Photography/Getty Images; 22: Stefan Auth/Media Bakery; 23: Keren Su/China Span/Alamy Images; 24: Iberfoto/Superstock, Inc.; 25: coolbiere photograph/Getty Images; 26: Dennis Cox/Alamy Images; 27: Victor Paul Borg/Alamy Images; 28: Vogel/Shutterstock, Inc.; 29 left: imageBROKER/Superstock, Inc.; 29 right: Dennis Walton/Getty Images; 30: zhouyousifang/Getty Images; 32: Blend Images/Alamy Images; 33: Mim Friday/Alamy Images; 34: Jon Bower Tibet/Alamy Images; 35: Patrick Horton/Getty Images; 36: Duncan Usher/ardea.com/Pantheon/Superstock, Inc.; 37: Abeselom Zerit/Shutterstock, Inc.; 38: SergeBertasiusPhotography/Shutterstock, Inc.; 39: NaturePL/Superstock, Inc.; 40: Feng Wei Photography/Getty Images; 42: Leisa Tyler/Getty Images; 44: akg-images/The Image Works; 46: Christopher Tozer/Alamy Images; 47: Chronicle/Alamy Images; 49: Heritage/Superstock, Inc.; 50: INTERFOTO/Alamy Images; 52: Alain Le Garsmeur Tibet Archive/Alamy Images; 54: imageBROKER/Superstock, Inc.; 55: GMPhoto/Alamy Images; 56: epa european pressphoto agency b.v./Alamy Images; 57: Christopher Tozer/Alamy Images; 58: Chinatopix/AP Images; 60 top: İsmail Çiydem/iStockphoto/Thinkstock; 60 bottom: Irina Rumyantseva/Shutterstock, Inc.; 61: Xinhua/Alamy Images; 62 left: Keith Levit/Design Pics/Superstock, Inc.; 64: Lucas Vallecillos/V&W/The Image Works; 65: Jitendra Singh/Getty Images; 66: Nadine Menezes/Alamy Images; 67: Pacific Press/Getty Images; 68: dpa picture alliance/Alamy Images; 70: STRDEL/AFP/Getty Images; 71: Lucas Vallecillos/age fotostock; 72: Peter Parks/Getty Images; 74: Singhanart/Shutterstock, Inc.; 75: Steve Allen Travel Photography/Alamy Images; 76: imageBROKER/Superstock, Inc.; 77: Agencja Fotograficzna Caro/Alamy Images; 78: Blaine Harrington III/Alamy Images; 80: STR/Getty Images; 83: John Henshall/Alamy Images; 84: David Lassman/The Image Works; 87: imageBROKER/Superstock, Inc.; 89: Michael Runkel/imageBROKER/Superstock, Inc.; 90: China Photos/Getty Images; 92: Michael Runkel/robertharding/Superstock, Inc.; 94: Vito Arcomano Photography/Alamy Images; 95: China Photos/Getty Images; 96: robertharding/Superstock, Inc.; 97: robertharding/Superstock, Inc.; 98: Marka/Superstock, Inc.; 100: John Lander/Alamy Images; 101: View Stock/Getty Images; 102: Melanie Stetson Freeman/Christian Science Monitor/The Image Works; 103 left: imageBROKER/Superstock, Inc.; 103 right: Stock Connection/Superstock, Inc.; 104: Tony Rowell/Alamy Images; 106: J Marshall - Tribaleye Images/Alamy Images; 107: Sbukley/Dreamstime; 108: Christophe Boisvieux/Superstock, Inc.; 109: Ashwini Bhatia/AP Images; 110: T. Kopecny/Alamy Images; 111: Ben Hider/Getty ImagesGetty Images; 112: epa european pressphoto agency b.v./Alamy Images; 113: Gesang Dawa/Xinhua/AP Images; 114: epa european pressphoto agency b.v./Alamy Images; 115: Channel Island Pictures/Alamy Images; 116: dbimages/Alamy Images; 118: Hemis/Alamy Images; 119: D and S Photographic Services/Shutterstock, Inc.; 120: Dani Salvà/V&W/The Image Works; 121: M. Watson/ardea.com/Pantheon/Superstock, Inc.; 122: Boaz Rottem/Superstock, Inc.; 123: Norma Joseph/Alamy Images; 124: Stock Connection/Superstock, Inc.; 127: Xinhua/Alamy Images; 130 left: Keith Levit/Design Pics/Superstock, Inc.; 131 bottom: Panorama Images/The Image Works; 131 top: Irina Rumyantseva/Shutterstock, Inc.; 132 top: coolbiere photograph/Getty Images; 132 bottom: Singhanart/Shutterstock, Inc.; 133 top: China Photos/Getty Images; 133 bottom: epa european pressphoto agency b.v./Alamy Images.

Maps by Mapping Specialists.